Badal Sircar

People's Playwright

Shailaja B. Wadikar

ATLANTIC
PUBLISHERS & DISTRIBUTORS (P) LTD

Published by
ATLANTIC
PUBLISHERS & DISTRIBUTORS (P) LTD
7/22, Ansari Road, Darya Ganj, New Delhi-110002
Phones : +91-11-40775252, 23273880, 23275880, 23280451
Fax : +91-11-23285873
Web : www.atlanticbooks.com
E-mail : orders@atlanticbooks.com

Branch Office
5, Nallathambi Street, Wallajah Road, Chennai-600002
Phones : +91-44-64611085, 32413319
E-mail : chennai@atlanticbooks.com

Printed in India at Nice Printing Press, A-33/3A, Site-IV, Industrial Area, Sahibabad, Ghaziabad, U.P.

To
Dr. Achyut Ban
and
Dr. Varsha Ban

Preface

> Voyages in the theatre. To go out there and come back and report. Talk to others about it, talk to myself about it. Go out again—with others, to others. Learn to speak to others, learn to listen to others. Try out things. Learn by doing.

So feels Badal Sircar, one of India's major playwrights, the pioneer of People's Theatre. There are the lines he accepted once and forever in the creation of his theatre. To make theatre reach to common man is his sole aim as a playwright and successfully he plods homewards his enthusiastic way. Theatre, for him, becomes an abode that has accommodated his cherished talent and aspirations and to which he has devoted his entire life to actualize his dream of establishing a just, humane, and equitable society.

Sircar is the leader of theatre-world in the true sense since he calls upon people to go hand in hand to discuss the current issues, to write a script, to make an ample use of human body as the most effective tool in presentation, to have a rigorous training and practice too, and finally to perform a play without the expectation of monetary gain. He is a playwright, director, theorist, teacher, mentor, and social activist having "visions and re-visions". The beacon, he showed, changed the theatre-goers' conventional sensibility of perceiving a play.

Though his plays are rooted in the specific language and location, they have varied invisible hues. If one delves deep into the core of the play, one gets exposed to his cosmopolitan discernment and concern for humanity. His theatre imparts a new dimension and vision to the writers, directors, performers, and spectators across the globe. It renders them thought-provoking and sensitive towards the complex issues that remain unsettled even in the contemporary society.

The corpus of works under study consists of the translated plays of Sircar. Among them, *Evam Indrajit, Baki Itihas, Pagla Ghoda, Shesh Nei,* and *Spartacus* are termed as the proscenium plays while *Procession, Bhoma, Stale News, Indian History Made Easy, Life of Bagala, Scandal in Fairy Land,* and *Beyond the Land of Hattamala* as the non-proscenium plays. In the earlier plays, Sircar follows the conventional mode in writing as well as in the performance and in the later, he invented new strategies in script writing and performance. Here, a sincere attempt has been made to make the spectators active participants. However, these are not the water tight compartments, as some of the proscenium plays are later on performed as the non-proscenium too.

"Looking into the Past" dwells on the analytical study of the pre-independence and the post-independence Indian English theatre, followed by the critical evaluation of the contribution of Sircar's contemporary playwrights: Vijay Tendulkar, Girish Karnad, and Mohan Rakesh.

"Bengali Theatre: Its Voyages" deals with a cursory survey of the various phases in Indian theatrical scenario with a focus on realism in Bengali theatre. It also illustrates how Badal Sircar's theatre is distinct from that of his predecessors', particularly, the theatre of Utpal Dutt.

Evam Indrajit proves to be a milestone in the history of modern Indian theatre as its protagonist Indrajit, like John Osborne's Jimmy Porter, becomes a spokesman of the 1960s' angry, frustrated post-war generation. The play ends with a message that all of us are the "cursed spirits of Sisyphus," and can do nothing but to continue our journey on this endless, weary way.

Calcutta Trilogy, that is, the group of three plays *Baki Itihas*, *Tringsha Shatabdi*, and *Shesh Nei* is the output of Sircar's contemplation on the effects of atom bomb. Each of them deals with the brutal absurdities of life, the terrible effects of nuclear weapon on society, aspirations and frustrations of the ruthless urban generation, its lack of concern and insensitivity to the environment that is going more and more critical. Invoking the voice of conscience the play *Baki Itihas* leaves the audience restless for being apathetic to the fact that oppression, murder, violence, war will be continued in the world as long as common human beings remain indifferent to the other side of history. The play *Shesh Nei* can be seen as a prelude to Sircar's shift from the proscenium to the non-proscenium theatre. Looking into inner-self, the spectators become restless about—their direct or indirect participation in spreading the tempo of terror and injustice—the issue that Sircar continues to tackle later on in his Third Theatre.

Pagla Ghoda occupies a unique place in Sircar's canon since it is the only play where women stand as a class. Throughout the play, there is a powerful plea to treat women as human beings. The image of 'pagla ghoda' symbolizes woman's untamed passion of love. All the male characters appear to be the culprits adopting the usual track in love-making of enjoying and then escaping.

The land-marking play *Spartacus*, based on the story of the great revolt of slaves took place in BC 71 that shook the mighty Roman Empire for four long years, shows Sircar's successful voyage from the proscenium theatre to Anganmancha. It is an open-ended play with a message "But the war of the oppressed against those who oppressed them went on...." Spartacus, the dead hero, becomes the phoenix for the slaves in the world forever since throughout the play the whispering of the slaves: "I'll return again in millions and millions" remains audible to the audience. Its transformation into a crescendo of assertion shows the submersion of the "I" into the unified "WE".

"From the Proscenium Theatre to the Third Theatre" comprises the detailed analysis of Sircar's shift from the conventional theatre to the non-proscenium theatre in order to bridge the gulf between the audience and the actors. Sircar thinks that the audience should be in direct touch with the actors and this he concretizes through his Third Theatre or People's Theatre.

The play *Procession* is an authentic montage on the monstrous and marvellous city of Calcutta. Actually, it is the extension of *Evam Indrajit.* Khoka is Indrajit's alter ego and the Old Man performs the same role as that of the Writer. Indrajit says: "....It won't ever get completed. Its end is its beginning." And its end has found a new beginning in *Procession.* The play shows the strength of a collective voice raised in the search of a real home as a revolt against the unjust, inhuman, ruthless system. Khoka, who has no longer any belief in a procession, becomes the part of it, as it is the procession to show a way to home.

A totally absurd play *Bhoma* illuminates the contradictions and disparities of the socio-economic situations in the society around. Here, the arguments and events have no continuity. But all of them reflect that the basic cause of poverty in life is exploitation, resulted out of lovelessness and lack of sympathy for fellow human beings. The image of poisonous trees refers to the class of exploiters. The play's end with Bhoma cutting down the poisonous trees accompanied by a group shows his victory over the evil forces.

Stale News links the past and present together to bring to notice the fact that conditions have not changed fundamentally even today and that the victim-victimiser relationship is the permanent relationship in pre- and post-independence Indian society. The play is full of violence, massacre and sensationalism, but it ends on an optimistic note with the young man provoking the people to raise a voice of protest against the capitalist society.

Indian History Made Easy is Sircar's comment on the unchanged miserable condition of the Indian peasants and the agricultural labourers after centuries of rule by various kings and governments and even in the post-independence era. Now the place of the East India Company is taken by "Mother Dollar". That is why the bourgeois class in India enters into a new alliance, this time with the "Mother Dollar".

The three plays *The Life of Bagala, Scandal in Fairyland* and *Beyond the Land of Hattamala* are based on the light-hearted fairytale. However, each of them gives a rational message. *The Life of Bagala* shows how constant humiliation reduces one's life to slavery and generosity helps one to regain self-confidence. *Scandal in Fairyland* exposes the ugly face of commercialism entered in the field of media which now becomes a fairyland of never-ending scandals. *Beyond the Land of Hattamala* throws light on Sircar's concept of an ideal society, his utopia, "where each gets according to his needs and each according to his ability."

Theatre, for Sircar, is a means of social reform. To make it people-oriented, he introduced new strategies in script-writing and performance. He is not just the vanguard of theatre but himself is a complete theatre!

Shailaja B. Wadikar

Contents

Introduction

In the post-independence era, the modern Indian dramatists have given a new, avant-garde type of drama with existential overtones. Within them, Badal Sircar forms a theatre within himself. Unlike several other playwrights, his focus is not on the writing of play but on its performance, that is, on the creation of theatre. He has made his stand very clear by stating: "I prefer doing theatre to writing theatre. Writing is quite laborious for me."

To change the world into a place worth of living seems to be the sole motto of Badal-da's life. Following the dictum: "Rest not till the goal is achieved," he worked calmly, quietly, patiently, tirelessly but confidently in the decided direction. He is not under the illusion that the disparity in life can be removed simply through theatre. However, he firmly believes that theatre can be one of the many facets of a movement that is vitally needed to bring about the expected revolution.

For Sircar, if theatre is used as a means of social reform, communication should not be one-sided, that is, what generally happens in the case of majority of plays. Instead, it should be a joint venture, a constant flow of give-and-take and sharing of ideas between the theatre-makers and the spectators. With this aim in mind, he walks constantly with people, encouraging them to actively participate in the performance of the play. His is the "People's Theatre" in the true sense of that word.

Enlightenment remains Sircar's major concern in his theatrical career. Naturally, the question of buying and selling of tickets has little or no consideration at all. A play without sets, props, costumes, mechanical devices like tape-recorders and projectors is

Sircar's Third Theatre. Human body is used as the indispensible element here. Having faith in living in community, Sircar makes people to join him in writing, directing and performing plays. The ultimate upshot of it is that he succeeds in transforming the spectators into the participants in play's action. This theatre now has a firm grip on their psyche to have a desired effect. It created within the audience a sense of community, that is, of "we" as opposed to "them" of the establishment.

Sircar devoted all his energies to the cause of social reform. Establishment of egalitarian society was his dream which finds manifestation in his play *Beyond the Land of Hattamala*. It is a humane society where all people lead life following the Marxian principle of combined effort "each according to his need and each according to his capacity".

Each of his plays takes the audience on a ride as if it is a voyage into the inner-self; it renders them introspective and thereby creates spaces for the transformation of their mind-set.

The present book *Badal Sircar: People's Playwright* comprises a comprehensive study of the Badal Sircar Theatre. It will flash like a light-house for the younger generation while understanding, accepting, appreciating and following Sircar's ideas in the march towards a humane social order, that is, an egalitarian society based on the principle of equality and social justice.

Shailaja B. Wadikar

Prologue

1

Looking into the Past

Theatre marks a radical change in the middle of the nineteenth century due to the publication of Darwin's land-marking book *Origin of the Species* published in 1859. The book challenges the established norms and concepts and gives rise to the naturalistic movement which has its profound impact on all branches of knowledge such as arts, history, culture, criticism, theatre along with science. The day-to-day life of common man and his problems become the themes of the literary works. Situations from actual life find expression in literature. It, therefore, becomes naturalistic. The Euro-American playwrights such as Ibsen, Shaw, Galsworthy, Barker, Sean O'Casey, T.S. Eliot, Tennessee Williams, Arthur Miller, Eugene O'Neill, Edward Albee, etc., impart a remarkable contribution to the tradition of realistic plays with their innovative ideas and strategies. All these Euro-American playwrights illustrate in their plays the deficiencies of modern man and the meaninglessness of contemporary life.

Theatre is used by these playwrights not as a means of amusement but as a means of changing the mind-set of people and thereby bringing a social reform. They set out to let something new that will disturb the audience and make them sensitive and introspective to the issues of day-to-day life. The plays are left open-ended for the spectators to ponder over the situation and to find out their own solutions and remedies to the problems discussed.

The plays of Ibsen, Shaw, Galsworthy, etc., come to be recognized as problem plays or plays of ideas. However, the term has been first used by E.M.W. Tillyard in connection with such plays of Shakespeare as *Measure for Measure, All's Well That Ends Well, Troilus and Cressida,* and *Hamlet,* since they deal with the dark aspect of human life and nature.

The French novelist Emile Zola has emphatically declared that only naturalistic movement can give vigour, life and novelty to the theatre. Henrik Ibsen, the famous Norwegian dramatist, uses drama to ask questions rather than to provide answers. His Nora becomes a role-model for the women in society. The life portrayed in his plays is as real as to be inevitable. In his plays, George Bernard Shaw aims at giving expression to the crude banality of everyday life.

The characters in Ibsen's plays bring to notice the burning reality of life that those who have the capacity first to see, understand, and accept the world as it is and then try to change it, can only achieve freedom and liberty. The weaker are ruthlessly crushed by the stronger in this fiercely competitive society. The protagonist of the play Nora slams the door not only of her own home but of all homes that seem happy and charming outwardly. So, her revolt against her husband takes her and all the audience away from the traditional notion of home, sweet home. It is for the first time that a womanly woman tries to face the burning, naked realities of actual world that is full of hardships and challenges. Her revolt has a profound influence on the British as well as the Indian playwrights. However, the popularity of the problem play is challenged by John Osborne's epoch-making revolutionary play *Look Back in Anger* opened at the Royal Court Theatre in London on 8th May 1956 that gives release to the feeling of anger and frustration. The protagonist of the play Jimmy Porter becomes the spokesman of the post-war generation as the youths of the age try to find in him the expression of their own feelings. A young graduate at the British university, running a sweet-stall to make a living, quite away from the comforts of the society is the true representative of the misfits of the welfare state.

Another trend that got popular in the decade of 1960s is 'absurd'. In 1961, Martin Esslin published his book *Theatre of the Absurd* and now the term is used for the plays of such playwrights as Samuel Beckett, Eugene Ionesco, Arthur Miller, Edward Albee, etc. These playwrights believe that human life is essentially irrational, illogical, out of harmony the result of which is the unceasing state of uncertainty, anguish and depression. The absurd plays permit irrational, illogical, and absurd events to happen on stage to bring out their central concern that this is the true nature of human life.

All these trends of Euro-American theatre are used successfully by Vijay Tendulkar, Girish Karnad, Badal Sircar, and Mohan Rakesh. The plays of each of them directly discuss the problems of contemporary life without trying to moralize or philosophize them. The spectators are provoked to think over the critical situation. Man is left in the midst of complexities. However, the term "problem play" cannot be used for their plays because what they project is not just a social problem but an aspect of our socio-political and cultural life mostly on psychological level. Their plays such as *Ghashiram Kotwal, Hayavadana, Bhoma, Half Way House*, etc., actually chart the course of avant-garde Indian theatre in the post-independence period.

The growth and development of Indian English drama can be studied period-wise and language-wise as: (i) pre-independence Indian drama and post-independence Indian drama, and (ii) the plays originally written in English and the plays translated into English. It is observed that in Indian literature, drama in English could not register a noticeable growth in the pre-independence period. English was a foreign language, and therefore, it was rather difficult to use it as a medium of creative writing and as well as to perceive, understand and accept by the spectators. The playwrights found it difficult to write natural, elegant, and refined dialogues in English and most of the English plays remained lacking in spontaneity.

Pre-Independence Indian English Drama

Majority of the plays in the pre-independence period deal with theme of east-west encounter. The beginning of Indian English drama is made by Krishna Mohan Banerjee with his play *The Persecuted* in 1831. It presents the conflict between tradition and modernity, that is, Indian orthodox thought and the new Western ideas and views. Michael Madhusudan Dutt's play *Is This Called a Civilization?* handles the questions of the contemporary day-to-day life of common people. Other playwrights of this period are A.S.P. Ayyar, T.P. Kailasam, J.M. Lobo Prabhu, S. Fyzee-Rahamin, K.R.S. Iyengar, D.K. Roy, Mrinalini Sarabhai, Sri Aurobindo, Harindranath Chattopadhyaya and Rabindranath Tagore. Among these, Aurobindo, Chatopadhyaya, and Tagore are considered to be "the big three" who have made a substantial and extensive contribution to the development of the Indian English drama. The only woman playwright of this period that seems to be worth considering is Bharati Sarabhai, the follower of Mahatma Gandhi and Jawaharlal Nehru. In her famous play *The Well of the People*, she depicts the theme of untouchability, the most burning problem of the then contemporary society.

Harindranath Chattopadhyaya's plays can be categorized as devotional plays, social plays, historical plays and miscellaneous plays. To mention a few of them are *Raidas, Tukaram, Chokhamela, Eknath, Pundalik, Sakubai, Jayadeva, The Window*, *The Parrot*, *The Sentry's Lantern*, *The Coffin, The Evening Lamp, The Burden*, *Fulfilment*, *The Purpose*, etc. The epics, the *Ramayana* and the *Mahabharata* become the source of the plots for his plays. He also writes some historical plays. Compassion for the victimized and oppressed people, revolt against the established outdated and useless norms of morality, and the evil forces of colonialism are the themes of his plays. Majority of the plays are of social nature which aims at projecting the contemporary social situation. It is for this reason that Iyengar has referred to his plays as: "manifestoes of the new dawn of realism." (Dharan 21)

It is observed that Sri Aurobindo's play-writing is highly influenced by the Shakespearian tragedy, the Jacobean tragedy, the Bible, and classical Sanskrit literature. One could easily notice his depth and proficiency in the great classics of Greece, Rome, France, Spain, and in the rich Sanskrit Literature. However, the most famous and the longest play *Perseus, the Deliverer* is inspired by his participation in the freedom struggle of India. The play explores the anguish, torture, hardships, and sufferings of freedom fighters. It is highly symbolic in nature in which Andromeda represents Mother India and Perseus is her rescuer. Some of his important plays are *Vasavadutta* (1957), *Rodogune* (1958), *The Viziers of Bassora* (1959) and *Eric* (1960). They have a variety of themes and well-designed structure but most of them are closet dramas.

Rabindranath Tagore's plays are grouped as (a) symbolic, (b) devotional, and (c) problem plays. Some of his earliest plays are *Sanyasi* (*The Ascetic,* 1884), *The King and the Queen* (1889), *Sacrifice* (1890), *Chitra* (1892), *Karna and Kunti* (1897) and *Gandhari's Prayer* (1897). He first used to write the plays in Bengali; later, himself translate them into English. However, his broadly celebrated plays *The Post Office* (1914) and *The King of the Dark Chamber* (1914) in Bengali were translated into English, by Devabrata Mukhopadhyaya and K.C. Sen respectively. The plays *Ascetic* and *Sacrifice* expose the social evils in which he condemned the sacrifice of people by accepting outdated customs and traditions. Tagore was greatly impressed by Kalidasa, Shakespeare, and Ibsen and tried to follow their modes and techniques in his plays. His versatile writing also contains a number of romantic playlets based on the Buddhist themes. They are *Malini* (1912), *The Worship of the Dancing Girl* (*Natir Puja* 1926), and *The Untouchable Girl* (*Chandalika,* 1933).

Post-Independence Indian English Drama

Mahesh Dattani, an actor, a director, a dancer, and a teacher is basically a contemporary Indian playwright writing originally in English. His plays boldly discuss the tabooed themes of sexuality, homosexuality, lesbian relationship, crime, horrible diseases like AIDS, as well as they deal with the sensitive issues such as religion, communal violence, feminine identity, etc. In 1998, he won the Sahitya Akademi Award for his play *Final*

Solutions and Other Plays. His remarkable contribution to Indian English theatre is noticed from his *Collected Plays* in two volumes. The first volume comprises such plays as *Seven Steps Around the Fire*, *On a Muggy Night in Mumbai*, *Final Solutions and Other Plays*, *Tara*, *Dance Like a Man,* etc. and the second one consists of the plays as *Thirty Days in September*, *Clearing the Rubble*, *Mango Souffle*, *The Swami and Winston*, *Morning Raga*, *Uma and The Fairy Queen*, *Ek Alag Mausam* and *The Tale of a Mother Feeding Her Child.*

Apart from the strong social sense, Dattani also possesses a deep passion and love for music and dance which is noticed in his plays *Dance like a Man* and *Morning Raga*. Being himself a stage performer, actor and director, he lays stress on theatricalities and the performance of the actor.

Two major women writers in this period who made a notable and striking contribution to Indian theatre are Manjula Padmanabhan and the Jnanpith Awardee playwright Mahasweta Devi. As a social activist, Mahasweta Devi has devoted her life to the cause of upliftment of the Dalits, Adivasis, and tribals. Her plays show her dedication and anxiety for the downtrodden sections of society who are deprived of their basic rights. Among her several plays, *Mother of 1084* (a novel, later on converted into drama), *Aajir*, *Bayen* and *Water* are worth noticing.

Manjula Padmanabhan's play *Harvest* won the Onassis Award and gave her recognition as the playwright of international repute. The play portrays the horrible world in the metropolitan city of Mumbai where mothers do not hesitate at least to sell their children for the sake of handful of rice. She has also written five monologues published in a volume titled *Hidden Fires*. They highlight the burning reality of the so-called modern contemporary life.

Other important playwrights in this phase who have contributed in their own ways to the growth and development of Indian English Drama are M.V. Rama, Santha Rama Rau, M. Krishnamurti, K.S.R. Sastri, D.M. Borgaonkar, V.K. Gokak, Nagarajan, Shiv K. Kumar, V.D. Trivedi, Ahmed Akhtar, Dina Mehta, Arati Nagarwalla, K.S. Rangappa, Murlidas

Melwani, Dilip Hero, P.S. Vasudev, Syed Amanuddin, Masti Venkatesa Iyengar, Utpal Dutt, Badal Sircar, Girish Karnad, Adya Rangacharya, Chandrasekhar Kambar, Chandrashekhar Patil, N. Ratna, Chandrakantha Kusnoor, P. Lankesh, Sriranga, G.B. Joshi, Mohan Rakesh, C.T. Khanolkar, Sadanand Rege, Amol Palekar, Vijay Tendulkar, Satish Aleker, Mahesh Elkunchwar, Vijaya Mehta, Sai Paranjape, etc.

In the pre-independence period, several European touring companies came to India and performed plays in Bombay for the growth of English drama. Many amateur groups and clubs flourished during 1860 and 1870, however, for the time-being. They could not provide a substantial and extending contribution since most of the plays were comedies, farces, operas that were not in harmony with the contemporary mood of the people. Noteworthy though the efforts are, they could not contribute to the growth of English drama in India. Contrary to the expectation, these activities remained helpful to the strengthening of the regional language theatres such as Marathi and Gujarati. English drama failed even to accept the challenge of the vernacular language drama. The ultimate upshot of it was the decline of English drama in India in the pre-independence period.

The development of the Indian drama originally written in English remained poor in the pre-independence period. However, in the post-independence period, the translated plays of such playwrights as Vijay Tendulkar in Marathi, Girish Karnad in Kannada, Badal Sircar in Bengali, and Mohan Rakesh in Hindi contributed a lot to the growth, progress, and expansion of theatre. Their plays chart the course of avant-garde Indian theatre in the scenario of the post-1960.

Sircar's Contemporaries

It is observed that dramas written in regional Indian languages and in their English translations have achieved a unique place in the theatrical world. In this modern era, the cultural interaction comes to be recognized as a significant factor in shaping the society. In order to connect the two globes and make the foreign readers familiar with Indian tradition and culture, there is a need for English translation of literature in the Indian languages. Playwrights like Vijay Tendulkar, Girish Karnad, Badal Sircar, and Mohan Rakesh have made bold experiments. They are set out to introduce new, tabooed subjects to shock the sensibility of the conventional readers. Their main object is to change the mind-set of the people and make them conscious of the harsh realities of their own lives.

Vijay Tendulkar

Vijay Tendulkar has been the most influential dramatist and theatre personality in the whole of Marathi literary culture who later on also won the international recognition with his play *Ghashiram Kotwal*. His career as a journalist gives him the opportunity to come across all kinds of violence and evils in society which he exposes in the plays like *The Vultures* (Gidhade, 1971), *Ghashiram Kotwal* (1972), *Sakharam Binder* (1972), etc. He is the avant-garde playwright who has an unconventional attitude towards contemporary human condition. The plays *Silence! The Court is in Session*, *The Vultures, Sakharam Binder,* and *Ghashiram Kotwal*, dealing with the theme of sex, violence, and sensation, have created a storm in the society. Each of them is considered his tour de force and a specimen of Marathi theatre of anger, violence and cruelty. The uproar that arose after the performances of these plays was a clear proof of their being new and unconventional.

The first play that marks the distinct individuality of Tendulkar from that of the Marathi dramatists of the earlier generation is *Manus Nawache Bet* (An Island Called Man). It gives him the recognition as a new playwright not only of the regional Marathi theatre but of the Indian theatre as a whole. In most his plays, he portrays the middle-class society, in which he depicts a man in conflict with society. The plays explore the contemporary problems that are discussed thoroughly and at length without giving any remedy. The main purpose of the dramatist is to make the people conscious of their own problems and to find out solutions for them. Like Brecht, he aims to create an epic theatre that demands the emotional detachment of the spectators in the action of the play. The plays are thought-provoking since they enable the audience to think rather than to passively accept the situation offered. A man is presented in the midst of complexities. The dialogues are short, incomplete, jerky and half-finished. But they designate more than what they say: For that, one needs to read between the lines, therefore!

The play *Silence! The Court is in Session* has earned him a place of honour among the leading Indian playwrights in the late sixties. It is based on a real-life incident. Tendulkar was asked to write the play for a competition. He received the stimulus from an amateur group on its way to stage a mock trial in a village near Mumbai. While over-hearing the conversation of the artists, the outline of the play takes place in his mind and the ultimate result of it is the creation of the play. It is a "play within a play" or a "play in the form of a rehearsal". The theme of the play is the victimization of an individual against society. It has raised several questions about moral values, love, sex, violence, the position of woman, etc. To expose the hollowness of the middle-class morality and dual standards of society, he makes ample use of irony, satire, humour and pathos. The success of the play lies in its universality. The questions raised by Benare, the play's protagonist, go beyond time and place. The play criticizes the society that punishes a woman very severely and let a man to go scot-free to commit more crimes. Benare is projected here as a rebel against the so-called established values of the male-dominated society. In this regard, she, like Nora, may be seen as a "New Woman" in the Indian context.

Tendulkar's name is associated with sex and violence after the performance of the play *The Vultures*. It is just due to the constant efforts and persuasion of Dr. Shriram Lagu that the performance could take place. According to Girish Karnad, "The staging of *Gidhade* could be compared with the blasting of bomb" (Banerjee xii). The conservative sections of Maharashtrian society got stunned by the open display of the scene of violence and sexual relation that constitute the plot. The play exposes the sheer violence arising from selfishness, greed, and sinfulness. At the pivot of the play, is the middle-class family consisting of a father, his two sons, a daughter, his illegitimate son and a daughter-in-law. Hari Pitale, the father of the three sons Ramakant, Umakant, Rajaninath and a daughter

Manik, prospers in his business by cheating his brother. The two sons and the daughter follow their father's beaten track and become the victims of viciousness. Through the characters of Rama and Rajaninath, the playwright throws light on the kinder aspect of human nature. The tragedy of Rama and Rajaninath highlights the burning reality that virtue too suffers if accompanied by vice.

The play *Sakharam Binder* delves deep to investigate the complexities of human nature. Through the character of Sakharam and those of his kept women Laxmi and Champa, Tendulkar throws light on man's basic craving for physical lust, violence, and power. Sakharam does not believe in the institution of marriage and therefore, arranges contractual relationship with a woman deserted either by her husband or by the society. The first act deals with the relationship of Sakharam-Laxmi, the second one that of Sakharam-Champa and the third one deals with the triangular relationship of Laxmi-Sakharam-Champa. It is the positive achievement of the playwright that he remains a totally detached, objective observer in the portrayal of each character which is the combination of vice and virtue, strength and weakness. Laxmi who sounds weak, docile, sensitive in outward appearance, turns out to be vicious towards the end of the play; Champa who is gross, sensuous, and strong shows great generosity towards Laxmi while giving her shelter in her house and Sakharam, the outwardly rough and tough man emerges out to be a totally bewildered one after the murder of Champa. Each of them is abnormal in his or her own way. However, unlike the characters in the play *The Vultures* they are the victims of circumstances and not that of any inherent weaknesses.

The plays *Encounter in Umbugland* and *Ghashiram Kotwal,* are based on the specific incidents in the field of politics in Indian history. The first one is related to Indira Gandhi's regime and the second one to one of the incidents in the 18th century Peshwa regime. However, to be more precise both of them comprise Tendulkar's comment on power-politics.

Despite the fact that both the plays divulge the nature of the game of power politics, and reflect the political reality of India of a specific period, they differ completely from each other in terms of subject-matter and thematic concern. The play *Encounter in Umbugland* is a political allegory as the characters represent historical personages and the story reflects the political situation of India in the late sixties and the early seventies. Through the character of Vijaya, Tendulkar shows the emergence of a "New Woman". At the same, side by side the play consists of, quite implicitly, a critique on the field of media.

Ghashiram Kotwal that makes Tendulkar's place very secure in the international galaxy of playwrights, is based on a particular incident in the 18th century Peshwa regime. However, it is a classic that dissolves the boundaries between temporality and historicity. The context of the play is universal, for the characters like Ghashiram, Nana, and Gauri are symbolic and, hence, belong to all ages and societies. It ends on the message that Ghashiram is dead only as a person and that his role will be played by some another person. Nana, Ghashiram, and Gauri are the ancestors of power-politics that world will always supply and observation will always find. The play is rich in the use of the content as well as in the use of theatrical devices. Here, we find the three-fold tradition of Indian theatre, that is, the classical, the folk, and the modern.

Kamala is, again, a topical play based on a real-life incident in the field of journalism. One particular sentence in the news paper: "How much did master buy you for?" (34) catches Tendulkar's attention and becomes the source of his writing here. Ashwin Sarin, the then editor of *The Indian Express* purchased a girl from a rural flesh-market and presented her at the press conference. Using this real-life incident, Tendulkar throws light on the flesh market, the exploitation of woman in her own house and that of in society, the cut-throat competition in the success-oriented modern generation and the egoistic hypocrisy of the young journalist. Jaisingh Jadhav, the protagonist of the play is the true representative of the contemporary youths who are ready to sacrifice human values in the name of humanity itself.

Kanyadan is, perhaps, the most controversial of Tendulkar's plays. It is the play that brought him the honour of Saraswati Sanman (award) and simultaneously the label of anti-Dalit playwright. But as revealed by the playwright in the interview sought by the present author/researcher, Tendulkar in this play, represents the utter defeat of his own generation that tries to tread along the path of idealism.

Arun Athawale was looked upon as the spokesman of the angry young generation among the Dalits of the post-1970 India. Through his character the play gives release to the feeling of anger and frustration of the Dalit youths. The inhuman treatment that his wife Jyoti receives from him is a kind of revenge that he seeks on the upper-middle-class society for having humiliated and exploited his ancestors for centuries. So, the play deals with the psychological study of the social tensions caused by casteism in the Indian society side by side with the development of Jyoti's character from a simple, sensitive soft-spoken and highly cultured Brahmin girl into an assertive, determined hardened spouse of a Dalit poet. The play ends with her accusing her father that he has rendered her mentally crippled by his void, false idealism. The miserable life of Jyoti with Arun makes her father Nath realize the hollowness of his optimism. Bitter experiences of life turn the downright idealist into a disheartened realist.

Tendulkar's play *A Friend's Story* deals with the bold theme of lesbianism. It is based on Tendulkar's story *Mitra* which he had written in the mid-50s. The story is related to the actual life-story of a girl from the city of Pune and whom Tendulkar himself had seen performing a male role on the stage. The play's subject is rather bold when it got performed for the first time. Mitra is portrayed as one having physical hormonal imbalance. She is a lesbian. Neither her relatives nor the society help her to get rid of this physical deformity. Getting totally frustrated, she commits suicide. The adept handling of such 'forbidden' subject-matter, once again, proves the fact that Tendulkar is an avant-garde playwright.

Tendulkar, in all his plays, shows his extraordinary capacity of dealing with the variety of themes, situations and characters.

The individual against the society, man's thrust for power, existence of human flesh market in the 21st century, currents and cross-currents of the present-day politics, dehumanization of man in the so-called cultured society, man-woman relationship, woman's position in the society, re-interpretation of the historical episodes, existentialism, absurdity of life are a few to mention of them. His theatre is enriched by the variety of themes as well as that of forms. His skillful handling of the distinct forms such as classical Sanskrit, folk, naturalistic, absurd, satirical, etc., proves him to be the vanguard of Indian theatre. The gradual change in the theme and the structure of the play throws light on Tendulkar's creative genius in drama that remains unparalleled in the whole realm of Indian English theatre.

Girish Karnad

Karnad is known to Indian theatre as a playwright, director, actor, and film-maker. His theatrical voyage is culminated in winning the most prestigious Jnanpith Award in 1999. He has enriched the Indian cultural scenario by his precious contribution to art, literature, theatre, and the film world. The highest peak of his dramatic career will be the day when he wins the much-coveted Noble Prize for literature in the near future.

Karnad occupies a distinct place in Indian theatre for his technical experimentation and for handling a wide range of themes and subjects. Through the use of history, legend, myth, and folklore, Karnad realistically depicts the problems of the contemporary life in allegorical or symbolic terms. He mingles myth and reality, past and present and utilizes legendary and historical figures in an effort to carry his message of reforming the present society. It is noticed that with his theatre, the post-independence Indian drama has made a fresh ground both technically and thematically. Karnadian theatrical canon represented the problems of the modern man, the absurdity of life, man's eternal struggle to achieve perfection, etc. Like Brecht, Karnad rendered the audience into the active participants since his plays make them respond the situation portrayed intellectually.

The existentialist play *Yayati* (1961), originally written in Kannada, has the foundation of one of the tales in the *Mahabharata*. The play is based on the theme of responsibility. Karnad's originality lies in skilfully portraying the inspiration behind Yayati's ultimate choice. Yayati in the story of the *Mahabharata* realizes that desire does not come to an end with its fulfilment. So, he returns Pooru's youth. However, Yayati, in Karnad's play returns Pooru his youth due to his realization of the horror of his new life.

The play depicts the elder generation that spoils the future prospects of the younger generation by expecting too much from them. This was exactly what was happening to him; his parents were against his decision of going abroad. In this play, Karnad has successfully dealt with such issues as existentialism, man-woman relationship in the male-dominated society, caste, class, race, and gender consciousness, sense of alienation, complexities of expectations and responsibilities. The women characters in the play Devayani, Sharmistha, and Chitralekha, represent the free and iron-willed women of society.

The play *Bali: The Sacrifice,* related to the Jain myth of the cock of dough, portrays the gulf between the two ideologies: violence and non-violence. It obliquely criticises the traditional, superstitious mind-set of Indian people who believe in rites and rituals. The King in the play is the follower of the *Shakti*-cult, which permits animal sacrifice. But when he marries a Jain girl, he is in love with, he accepts Jainism against his mother's wish. Later on, his queen plays false to her spouse and betrays her marriage vows by getting herself spoiled by the mahout. The King's mother asks him to sacrifice one hundred sheep for her purification. Being a Jain, the King refuses to do so. But later on, by a compromise, he agrees to sacrifice a batter-cock and compels the Queen to join him in this symbolic sacrifice. For the Queen, the intended violence is more dangerous than that of the actual one. So, she sacrifices her own life for the cause of her Jain religion.

The myth of Yavakri from the Vanaparva of the *Mahabharata* is the source of the play *The Fire and the Rain.* The play projects the conflict between the rigid, ritualistic, orthodox Brahmin community symbolised by fire and the life-giving, benevolent tribal community symbolised by rain. Fire destroys everything and rain sustains life. By means of the two myths one that of Yavakri and the other that of Indra, Karnad throws light on the universal themes of love, jealousy, revenge, violence, futility of knowledge, weakness of human nature and loneliness. The play communicates the message that abuse of knowledge ultimately leads to the destruction of the world. Although the themes of revenge, hatred, violence pervade the entire atmosphere, the play marks the triumph of goodness over evil. That is why it ends in rain.

In *Hayavadana,* Karnad has used the ancient myth of transposed heads to depict multiple themes of search for identity, incompleteness, love, mind-body dichotomy, social system and social norms. The play has two plots. Its main plot portrays the life story of Devadatta, Padmini, and Kapila while the subsidiary one deals with the fulfilment of Hayavadana's desire of achieving completeness. The earlier one is based on a story from the *Kathasaritasagara*, an ancient collection of stories in Sanskrit and on the German novella of Thomas Mann *The Transposed Heads*. On the surface level, the theme of the play is eternal love triangle, that is, two men in love with one woman. Three friends—Devadatta, Padmini, and Kapila occupy the centre of the story. Padmini marries Devadatta, but is gradually infatuated by Kapila's strong body. Her attraction becomes the cause of their ruin. Friendship is replaced by rivalry. Their relations get entirely tangled and ultimately the friends kill each other. Padmini's efforts of having a complete man as a life-companion, for which she transposes the heads of Devdatta and Kapila, of course, with the boon of the Goddess Kali, remain useless and she commits suicide. However, her desire of complete man gets fulfilled posthumously in her son.

The play *Hayavadana* communicates the message that no human being is complete by himself. The real cause of this incompleteness is the dichotomy between mind and body. *Hayavadana*, the horse-headed man, represents this physical incompleteness. The *intellectuals*, in their attempts to acquire knowledge, lose their body and the *shudras*, in their efforts to grow strong through physical exercise, lose their intellect. Head stands for intellectual attainments and body for that of physical pleasure. It is the head and not the body that confirms man's real identity. The character of Hayavadana becomes a complete horse, when Goddess Kali grants to fulfil his wish. What is more important between the two—the head or the body? is the question left for the audience's contemplation.

In *Nagamandala*, Karnad has narrated the folk-tale through story-telling. The play describes the marital life-story of Apanna-Rani with the intrusion of the Naga. The central issue of the play is Rani's fidelity to her husband, Appanna. Exercising complete supremacy over Rani, he locks her within the house and himself develops an illicit relationship with a concubine. On the suggestion of Kurudavva, Rani gets ready to try the love potion on her husband to win his love. But the blood-red colour of the potion leaves her scared and in a moment of disorientation she throws it off upon a nearby anthill. Naga drinks it and consequently falls in love with Rani. He starts visiting her at night in the form of Appanna. The love relationship results in Rani's pregnancy. Appanna, her husband, accuses her of infidelity. The village elders ask Rani to give a trial to prove her chastity. With the support of Naga; Rani gives the snake trial and successfully comes out of it. The entire village and her husband, too, honour her as goddess.

Thus, Rani's life-story represents the sexual oppression of women in the Indian society for ages. The play criticises the double standards of the society in which a woman is often punished very severely and man often goes unquestioned even unnoticed. The ordeal, on the day of judgement, exposes the gender-based values, morals, and injustice of our society.

The dramatic monologue *Flowers* has the basis of a folk-tale from the Chitradurga region of Karnataka. The story fundamentally deals with the metaphysical dilemma between *Dhárma* and *Kāma* which occupies the centre of human existence.

By using myths, legends, and folktales, Karnad has put forward the complications and predicament of modern individual.

Similarly, in some of his plays, he exploits history to interpret the contemporary life and its problems. Actually, Karnad treats history as a battleground for the discussion of the class, caste, racial controversies in the political field. The social reformer Basavanna in *Tale-Danda*, the medieval king Tughlaq in the play *Tughlaq* and the 18th century king of Mysore, Tipu Sultan in *The Dreams of Tipu Sultan* are the historical personages but in the course of time, they have gained a mythological status.

Tughlaq is undoubtedly one of the greatest plays of Karnad which symbolically exposes the hollowness of Jawaharlal Nehru's idealism. In his attempt of establishing an ideal kingdom, Tughlaq becomes a tyrant without being conscious of his tyranny. He kills his father and brother to acquire the throne and persecutes all those who oppose his plans. The idea that Karnad seems to put forth through this play is that the ruler's role of oppressor is the greatest obstacle in the way of his idealism. It represents nothing but his propensity for violence and destruction. The play is, thus, a critique on the drawbacks that reside in the minds of the rulers and the ruled. The central character of the play, though historical, its content and the concern have universal significance.

Tale-Danda also has a historical reference for the events depicted and the characters portrayed. However, this too is not a historical play. The historical events are closely linked up with social reformation of the "*Sharanas*" that took place in the twelfth century in Karnataka. Basavanna's fight against the inhuman caste-system occupies the centre of the play. The play upholds the values of work-culture and community-living. But unfortunately, Basavanna's sincere attempts to bring equality in all walks of life end in violence and massacre. Karnad, here, exploits history in order to expose intolerance and violence in the name of religion and at the same, he throws light on the socio-political ills and evils of the present society.

The play discloses the ugly face of the caste system prevalent in Indian society that cannot be abolished without a bloodless revolution. Both the rulers and the ruled favour its pervasiveness even at the cost of their life. All the efforts of Basavanna to remove the barriers of 'caste and class come to nothing, when he performs a marriage of a Dalit boy with a Brahmin girl. The battle that is ultimately fought by the *Sharanas* against the orthodox people culminates in the carnage and the plunder of their property by the royal army. The revolution, thus, ends in a great failure at the instance of the counter-revolutionary force, resulting eventually in the continuation of the old, status quoist order.

The play *The Dreams of Tipu Sultan,* is about the early days of colonialism in India. At the core of the plot is Tipu Sultan and his dreams in the last phase of his life. Using the events of the specific events of history as his material, Karnad has vividly dramatized Tipu's struggle for freedom and independence. This play, like *Tughlaq,* is enriched in the use of images, symbols which comprise various mysteries regarding the personality of Tipu Sultan.

The latest plays such as *Broken Images, Wedding Album, Boiled Beans on Toast* and *Driven Snow* (still unpublished in English) show Karnad's "criticism of life", i.e. his running commentary on the current social order.

In *Broken Images,* Karnad deals with the reality of the present time in the field of literature. Here, he discusses such issues as plagiarism, politics of language, supremacy of literary genre, and the question of identity. Actually, the replicated images on the screen symbolically represent the protagonist's voice of conscience, her alter-ego that renders her guilt-conscious and crushes her pride ruthlessly.

The play *Wedding Album,* contains the cultural degradation of Indian society and thereby exposes the Hindu fundamentalism that claims purity of race and culture in the Indian context. He very candidly inspects the hidden passions, lurking sexual desires that lie deep-rooted beneath apparent layers of cultural sophistication. The play is a burning criticism on the Hindu rituals and institutions such as marriage and family that are considered to be the holiest of holy in the Indian set-up. Observing the play seems like turning the photographs of Indian culture.

Karnad's recently published play *Boiled Beans on Toast* is the portraiture of the city of Bangalore. Although it has a mythological origin, it is Karnad's running commentary on the prevalent life in that city. Bangalore is particularly widely known for its massive cosmopolitan populace, its progress in IT, pleasant weather, cheap beer and heavy traffic. However, very little has been written, seen, heard, or noted about its average resident, that is, housewives, the non-IT professionals, labourers, senior citizens, the expatriates and others. This latest play whirls round the unsung tales of ordinary Bengaluru citizens and their struggle for existence.

Driven Snow is distinct from other plays since it is the only play with a non-Indian locale. It simultaneously explores the post-colonial society in two nations: England and India and throws light on the psyche of the non-resident Indians, especially of those who went to England with some aspirations in their minds and hearts. Karnad, here, very boldly portrays the sister-brother relationship which later develops into an illicit, nay, incestuous, one-sided love relationship. Side by side, the play throws light on the class-struggle in England and the caste-struggle in India.

To conclude, it can be said that the socio-political milieu in India finds a fine expression in artistic form in Karnadian canon. The plays encompass Karnad's criticism of life since they depict the vices, drawbacks, and limitations of the contemporary Indian society. One can easily notice in them his dislike for hypocrisy, barbarism, superficiality, narrow-mindedness, corruption, duplicity, treachery, and violence. While depicting the drawbacks and vices of both an individual and society, the playwright's concern for the betterment of society can be clearly perceptible.

Mohan Rakesh

Rakesh was a versatile writer, who successfully tried his hand at writing short stories, novels, and plays. In addition to these, he also had to his credit collection of essays, biographies and travelogues. He imparted a new life in whatever he wrote, but it is as a playwright that his work won him a lasting place in the literary galaxy. His first play *Ashadha Ka Ek Din* (*One*

Day in Ashadha) (1958) received the Sangit Natak Akademi Award for the best play in 1958. *Leheron Ke Rajhans* (*The Great Swans of the Waves*) (1963) and *Adhe Adhure* (*Half Way House*) (1969) were two other full-length plays which he wrote. In 1968, he was again honoured with the Sangit Natak Akademi for his excellence in the field of drama and his considerable and valuable role to its development. As recognition of his concern for the language of theatre, he received Nehru Fellowship to carry out research on 'the dramatic word'.

Mohan Rakesh's two translated plays, i.e., *One Day in Ashadha* and *The Great Swans of the Waves* are based on historical or semi-historical background while *Half Way House* is related to the issues of the modern society. All of them have an intimate link with the contemporary reality. The dialogues are natural, spontaneous, and are potent with meaning. The characters represent modern man's psychological conflict, frustration, dissatisfaction, and the resulting anger in a unique and unusual manner. The language of the plays differs radically from that of the early Hindi playwrights. The contemporaneity of the plays puts him on a higher level of competence.

The play *One Day in Ashadha,* having the legendary character of Kalidasa, focuses on the contemporary issues. The play brings to notice that the ideal concepts such as love, devotion, commitment, sincerity, etc., are beyond one's reach. The protagonist of the play Kalidasa, a sensitive playwright, cannot keep himself away from royal temptations. He marries the princess and betrays Mallika, his beloved, who is a perennial source of poetic inspiration for him.

In the play *The Great Swans of the Waves,* Rakesh depicts the dilemma of a modern man caught in the maze of mental conflict to be or not to be. Nand, the protagonist of the play can neither renounce life nor love it completely. Sundari represents love of life and Buddha that of renunciation of it. Being unable to make a sharp choice, Nand, emerges as a tragic character.

The play *Half Way House* has no story in the traditional sense. In the construction of the plot structure, it seems to have followed the traditional style, i.e., a play neatly divided into acts and scenes having beginning, middle, and end. It is absurd in the sense that there is no development of action. The play ends where it starts. The movement of the play is neither horizontal nor vertical; instead, it is circular, very subtle, and well-planned.

Here, Rakesh dealt with the theme of man-woman relationship. The play portrays the changing identity of women in the twentieth century. Being economically independent, she is trying to get the equal status in the making of family. Savitri, the protagonist of the play, is a new woman who struggles to find peace, joy, and happiness. Consequently, the play projects man-woman relationship which is fraught with tensions, dislikes, mutual suffocation, and alienation.

Rakesh's plays show the anger and commitment in the post-independence Indian theatre. They deal with the mental conflict, helplessness, frustration, dissatisfaction, and anger of the modern individual who can neither adjust himself with the fast-changing society nor can change it. Kalidas in *One Day in Ashadha,* Nand in *The Great Swans of the Waves,* Man I in *Half Way House* fail to accept the challenge of life and therefore, ran away from Mallika, Sundari, and Savitri, respectively. Whether their life-partners could outwit the odds in their respective lives is the question left for the audience's imagination and understanding of their deeds and misdeeds.

Rakesh in his plays, thus, explores "the modern man's failure to understand himself and others and their mutual failure to understand each other, which is the real tragedy of modern life." (Choudhari 512; qtd. in Manchi 24)

Badal Sircar

Badal Sircar appeared in the Indian theatre at an appropriate time when Indian drama was passing through the transition period. He introduced a new dramatic idiom in Bengali and later on in Indian theatre through his "Third Theatre". His plays illustrate the meaninglessness, absurdity of our existence that led to the state of anguish and depression. The society portrayed was the middle-class one and the questions he handled were politico-economic, socio-cultural, and psychological ones.

Sircar firmly believes that theatre is an instrument of social transformation. The span of his theatre can be divided into two phases: Proscenium and non-proscenium. His plays like *Evam Indrajit* (1962), *That Other History* (*Baki Itihas*, 1964), *There's No End* (*Shesh Nei*, 1971), and *Mad Horse* (*Pagla Ghoda*, 1967) belong to the proscenium and they deal with political, social, psychological and existential problems. Greatly influenced by the Russian playwright Grotowski's concept of 'Poor Theatre', Sircar formulated his 'Third Theatre'. Through it, Sircar reduces all the stage props like sets, costumes, lights, sound, etc., and lays stress on the use of "human body" as the most important tool. The focus of his plays in this phase is on the effect of lovelessness on society which ultimately leads to the exploitation and oppression of peasants, workers, villages and developing countries by landlords, industrialists, cities and advanced countries respectively. The Third Theatre includes such plays as *Procession* (1972), *Bhoma* (1974), *Stale News* (1979), etc. In *Beyond the Land of Hattamala,* Sircar puts forth his dream of egalitarian society where each individual will get according to his capacity and his own need. Sircar has attempted to revolutionize the Indian Theatre elevating it to the Euro-American drama. The influence of Sartre, Camus, and Grotowski is quite evident in the treatment of his themes and delineation of his characters.

Sircar's early plays express the meaninglessness of human existence that ultimately results in the state of anguish. The plays represent the alienated protagonist who can neither adjust themselves in the fast changing society nor possess the capacity to change it. The ultimate result of it is that they are left with the sense of guilt along with resultant frustration that disturbs or discomforts the audiences and makes them think a new and a fresh. This phase comprises such plays as *Evam Indrajit, That Other History, There's No End,* etc., which are based on political, economic, social, and cultural problems.

Like Brecht's Epic Theatre, his theatre also demands the emotional detachment on the part of the audience and therefore remains successful in creating the "Alienation-Effects" on its audience. The plays aim at producing a class of conscious audience who will ponder over the dilemma of the protagonists, and, in the process, they become self-aware and self-introspective.

The character of Indrajit, in the play *Evam Indrajit,* resembles the image of John Osborne's "angry young man". The play ends with his realization that he is not distinct from others and life remains the same in the foreign countries as in India. This consciousness leaves him hopeless and frustrated. Due to the existential overtones, the play belongs to the tradition of absurd plays. According to Eakambaram, "The play is an Indian version of *Waiting for Godot.*" (Babu 95)

Using the scenes of the Santhal Revolt in the British India, Sircar brings to notice through *Stale News* that social inequality, oppression, and exploitation are the inevitable features of the Indian society in all periods of our history. The situation in the British regime and in free India remains the same. The incidents in the play indicate that the Indian Government is as much oppressive in nature as that of the British Government since both of them exploit the people of the lower strata of society and remain in favour of those of the higher strata to protect their own political interests.

The play *That Other History* describes the storm and violence caused by the demon that lives within the mind of human being, not in the outer society. It also focuses on the guilt-consciousness of middle-class man for being indifferent to the social condition and his responsibilities. The protagonist of the play Sitanath tries to commit suicide. The motivation for suicide is not the personal tragedy but a total apathy of the middle-class to the dark side of history.

Sircar's another play *There's No End* represents a protagonist, that is, Sumanta in search of a meaningful life. For this, he goes on changing the ways of life but remains unsuccessful in all his efforts.

In the play *Procession,* Sircar represents the meaninglessness of human life. The so-called wonders, innovations, and development of science and technology such as the various means of entertainment, press, mass media, etc. make human life worthless. People are made mindless through nationalism, religion, education, and many other sources so that they can sustain the perpetuation of the exploitative and oppressive character of our culture.

In *Bhoma,* Sircar represents the dehumanized condition of life. Exploitation and oppression are the integral parts of it. The play communicates that you want others to love you but you yourself are not inclined to love others. The spiritual sterility depicted here is similar to that of one portrayed in *The Waste Land* by T.S. Eliot. Sircar is not happy by merely criticizing the status quoist forces here, but finds the real cause of misery lying in the lovelessness, apathy, and indifference shown to one another.

It is observed that Sircar's focus in his plays is not on a single individual but on the entire society. That is why each of his plays is a means of socio-political propaganda and, hence, by and large, seems to lack plot and characterization but carries a message of its own.

In the pre-independence period, Indian English drama goes on decline. But in the post-independence period, the decade 1960-70 invites attention since the regional drama acquires a national identity. The plays written in Hindi, Bengali, Kannada, and Marathi have been translated into English and other languages. These playwrights have a strong historical sense. That is why some of the plays have an intimate link with its roots, that is, the classical and the folk theatre. At the same, their plays are modern since they deal with the issues that belong to all times and climes. Contemporaneity is the hallmark of each of them. However, the theatre of each of the playwrights is distinct from that of the other. Tendulkar's approach of representing the burning reality is direct and straightforward; Karnad goes back to ancient folklore, legend, and history to depict reality in a symbolic way; Mohan Rakesh chooses the historical or semi-historical background to interpret contemporary life. And Sircar's Third Theatre is in true sense the "People's Theatre". What Erin B. Mee states in her Introduction to *Drama Contemporary* she has edited very well applies to the theatre of these playwrights: "I hope that each play will take people on a journey.... It can be a journey into one's self from a stance outside one's own cultural viewpoint." (Mee 18)

In the hands of these four playwrights, drama becomes a means of making people aware of the reality of their own lives. The plays leave the audience disturbed and introspective. These playwrights have made bold innovations in the theme, setting, stage direction, and costumes also. The effective handling of the neglected, forbidden subject matters shocks the sensibility of the conventional audience. Drama here is successfully used as a means of social reform. The playwrights' commitment to human values can be clearly perceived in their plays.

The effective use of the various traditions in the classical theatre and the folk theatre throws light on their high sense of tradition and their capacity to represent distinctly through them issues, questions relating to the contemporary modern society displays their individual talent.

In the final analysis, the art of these playwrights may be seen as a liberating influence. It broadens the ambit of thinking and conscience and enables one to become "human"—as human as possible.

Works Cited

Babu, Manchi Sarat. *Indian Drama Today*. Prestige Books, 1997.

Banerjee, Arundhati. Introduction. *Five Plays of Vijay Tendulkar*, by Vijay Tendulkar, OUP, 1992.

Choudhari, N. "Hindi Drama." *Comparative Indian Literature*, edited by K.M. George, Macmillan, 1984.

Dharan, N.S. *The Plays of Vijay Tendulkar*. Creative Books, 1999.

Mee, Erin B., editor. Introduction. *Drama Contemporary*. OUP, 2002.

2

Bengali Theatre: Its Voyages

> Voyages, not just one voyage. No final destination. Each port is a midway stop, the end of one lap of journey. The next port is ahead, another voyage is to be undertaken. Just as it happens in life.

So says Badal Sircar (*On Theatre* 91), the pioneer of Third Theatre that he creates for people. What follows here is a cursory review of the various phases in Indian theatrical scenario with a focus on the Bengali theatre.

Realism in Indian Theatre

Realism came into existence as a major tenet in Indian literature during the thirties of twentieth century, when a group of Indian students in London, joined together to form the Indian Progressive Writer's Association. This movement ultimately led to the formation of the All-India Progressive Writers' Conference at first at Lucknow in April 1936, and later at Calcutta, in 1938.

The main purpose of this conference was to initiate realism in literature and differentiate it from the traditional literature that had tried so far "to find a refuge from reality in baseless spiritualism and identity" (Pradhan 20). The movement soon becomes nation-wide and a host of progressive writers successfully tried to give expression to the basic problems of Indian society like hunger, poverty, social backwardness, political subjugation, etc. The endeavour was to arouse a critical spirit that would scrutinize existing institutions and customs in the light of reason, the motto being "to act, to organise ourselves, to transform." (Pradhan 21)

It is due to this movement that Indian writers came under the common umbrella of radical inspiration to introduce scientific rationalism in literature for the first time. The stress on realism consequently leads to arouse the questions regarding form and content in the composition of this new literature. However, the persistence at this stage was on "the truth of content" (Ali; qtd. in Sudhi 82) considering form and technique to be the unnecessary embellishments. And the idea that realistic literature was principally a literature of a new radical content was accepted both in theory and practice by most writers during this early phase. The ultimate upshot of this movement was the formation of the Indian People's Theatre Association, and Bengal was to take a leading part in both these movements.

This movement affected all genres of literature and Indian drama was not the exception. It tried to make theatre, "the experience and the organiser of our people's struggle for freedom. The main aim of theatre according to All-India Conference was recognized as to "enlighten" the masses about the nature and "solution" of the problems facing them through plays, ballads, and songs that "suited...the purpose in view" (Indian People's Theatre Association 129 and 131). It was also suggested and demanded that productions should be both simple as well as direct to make them easily 'intelligible' for people. This movement, in a short period of time had a grip on the psyche of people and came to be recognized as an effective, well-organised medium of mass-awakening. Slowly, the focus shifted to the themes of social exploitation, the struggle of workers, peasants and the middle class.

It is because of Indian People's Theatre Association (IPTA) that theatre gets released from its preoccupation with mythological, religious, and romantic gratification. The staging of Bijon Bhattacharya's *Nabana* in October-November 1944, by the Bengal unit of the IPTA, by both the author and the renowned Sambhu Mitra, was to assist for remodelling the theatrical idiom in Bengal. Dispensing with artificial sets and illusory effects, its theme was oriented towards depicting the filth and the anguish of the poor and depressed. An era of determined theatre had been heralded by the IPTA. However, this tempo of achievement was soon constrained by the emergence of a new political militancy that neglected the importance of the artistic composition of the work. This became a major cause of discord between Sambu Mitra and the members of the ballet wing.

After 1949, the Communist Party of India inflicted a rigid control over the functioning of the association. This diminished the national status of the IPTA making it merely a mouthpiece for party propaganda. Also due to the misunderstanding in the internal body (between the drama and the ballet wings) some playwrights who refused to compromise were unceremoniously dropped from circulation. Subsequently, the IPTA went through a severe setback and by, 1950 had lost its hold on the Indian cultural scene. (Ghose 304; qtd. in Pronoti 35)

In the initial phase, Bengali theatre was under the influence of the Marxist thought which led to instigate greater social awareness. However, due to the neglect of the coordinate relationship between the political tendency of the work and its literary technique, the artistic value, as well as the political impact of the work degraded. The insertion of an explicitly formulated message decreased the aesthetic quality of the work and it ultimately resulted in a vulgarisation of content. There also developed a feeling that theatre based on Western models somehow failed to produce the desired effect. As a reaction to it, the IPTA determined to change its strategy and concentrate more and more on forms of folk art in Bengal. This resulted in the revival of interest in forms like the Jatra in Bengal and was carried to a climax by artists like Utpal Dutt who emerged on the scene after the middle of the (twentieth) century. (Chukerbutty 37)

The present study aims to attempt Badal Sircar's contribution to the Indian theatre. He has his place very secure in the history of contemporary Bengali drama. Hence, it will be interesting to trace its growth and development in the present context—to see what theatre he did receive and what he sought to make of it.

Bengali Theatre: A Diachronic Survey

To begin with the beginning, theatre written and performed in Bengali language is referred to as Bengali theatre. At the very outset, it began as a form of private entertainment but later on played a pivotal role in manifesting dislike of the British rule in India in the pre-independence period. After independence, the leftist movement in West Bengal used theatre as a tool for social reform. This theatre in Bengali language at present exists in Bangladesh and the present eastern Indian states of West Bengal and Tripura.

The popular folk forms of Bengali theatre were Jatra, Alkap, Bahurupi, Chhau, Gambhira, Kabigan, Kathkata, Palagan, Panchali, Putul Nach, etc. Along with these folk forms, proscenium theatre was also originated and developed in Calcutta, the most significant city of the expanding British Empire in the East towards the end of the eighteenth century. The British administrators set up English theatre with the purpose of entertainment. At first, the performances were organised exclusively for the English and the Europeans; later, they were kept open for the Indians too. The plays, performed here, included those by Shakespeare, Oliver Goldsmith, and many other significant English writers.

The first play staged in Bengali theatre in 1795 and again in 1796 was *Kalpanik Sambadal* ('Imaginary Transformation'), a translation of the English play *The Disguise*. The play was directed and organised by a Russian musician with Bengali actors and actresses. However, it did not appear to have influenced the consequent events.

By 1830, a large and fast-growing class of affluent Bengali merchants, landlords, moneylenders, and professionals settled in Calcutta. English, for these educated people, became a window through which they could receive fresh ideas and knowledge. Getting influenced by these ideas, they became the ardent admirers of English literature and drama. The early patrons of theatre were the enlightened people of Bengali aristocratic class. They built stages in their palatial homes and gardens but put up shows exclusively for invited audiences. The first such endeavour came in 1831 and the second one in 1835. Since then no original Bengali drama was in existence; mostly Sanskrit classics in translation were staged. The first original Bengali play, *Kulinakulasarbaswa* (All about Kulin Clan) by Ramnarayan Tarkaratna criticising the Brahman practice of polygamy, was performed in 1857. The contemporary playwrights Michael Madhusudan Dutt and Dinabandhu Mitra imparted Bengali theatre the much-needed sustenance in 1860s.

The theatrical circle was enlarged by the joining of the new, emerging middle-class people, comprising lawyers, doctors, writers, educationists, traders, etc. However, in the writing and staging of plays, they tried to imitate the English ones. Similarly, Bengali theatre, in its earlier phase, could not get rid itself from the impact of Jatra. Though the English-educated Indian elite class mocked at this popular folk form outwardly, they could neither reject it nor remove its influence. Similarly, the private theatres of the wealthy provided a type of motivation to the amateur theatres started by the middle class in the north part of Calcutta. No doubt, the amateur theatres depended on the patronage of the well-to-do, but they too remained contributory to fulfil the rising demand for public theatres where the common citizen could get an entry.

Due to the widespread desire and demand of people, some active amateurs and other enthusiasts formed an association and established a play-house called National Theatre. Actually, the venue used was a hired part of a zamindar's mansion at forty rupees per month. The first play performed at this provisional auditorium on 7th December 1872, was Mitra's anti-British *Nildarpan* (Indigo Mirror) which received an overwhelming response. One show a week was scheduled and a few of which were organised before the National Theatre split up. The success and popularity in the initial stages proved to be an incentive for others to start public theatres at hired sites and temporary structures. The ultimate upshot of it was that they soon felt the need for permanent playhouses. With the collaborative efforts of all these amateurs and enthusiasts, the Bengali theatre was established and the first play performed in it on 16th August 1873 was Dutt's *Sharmishtha*. That women performed the female roles for the first time became the striking feature of this play. However, it could not be relished or even taken easily by the people since the actresses were from the red-light district. Nevertheless, the protest was short-lived and other contemporary companies followed the beaten track.

Meanwhile, some permanent venues got established in the same locality. The prominent among them were the Great National Theatre and Star Theatre. The formation of permanent playhouses designated two developments. One was the growth of theatre's popularity among the educated middle class and the other was the fact that theatre no longer needed the patronage of the rich. That the people started discussing the merits and demerits of acting and other aspects of production showing their alertness, discernment and knowledge was a praiseworthy quality.

The contemporary developments were in harmony with the expansion of theatre. Many dramatists emerged; there was an increase in the number of plays. In addition to it, the dramatization of novels, particularly, that of Bankimchandra Chatterjee's, and a few long narrative poems remained a fruitful source. But most of the new playwrights showed a little understanding of the nature and craft of drama with the exception of Jotirindranath Tagore. Majority of his plays were the translations of the Sanskrit classics and some of them were the adaption of a few comedies of his favourite, Moliere. However, to give them the feel of Bengali plays, he changed the names of the characters and locales. Others who contributed to this dramatic movement were Amritlal Basu, Manmohan Basu, Rajkrishna Ray, Girish Ghosh. Rabindranath Tagore, the versatile genius, also started writing his unique plays in the 1880s.

Still the corpus was not large sufficient to meet the rising demand for entertainment. That the educated class did not acknowledge or accept the influence of the vernacular was another problem. It still wanted theatre to follow copying Elizabethan dramatic structure. The profound influence of English theatre and that of the folk form Jatra became a big hurdle. The only remedy was to yoke them into a form that would be liked by the audience. Bengali theatre succeeded in outwitting the so-called difficulties because of Girish Ghosh. "He fused the ill-fitting combination into a distinct entity that answered to the Bengali genius and became the standard for many decades." (Lal 11)

The other artists who played a significant role in the early days of the Bengali theatre were Ardhendu Mustafi, Binodini Dasi, Amritalal Basu, Manmohan Basu, Sukumari Dutta, Amritalal Mitra, etc. All these first-rate actors and actresses, with their artistic calibre, kept the audience spellbound by providing them ecstatic joy, hearty laughter, and cathartic sorrow. In the first three decades, weekly shows increased; their appeal was reflected by the lively coverage in Bengali and English newspapers. However, by the end of the nineteenth century and with the beginning of the twentieth century, the average member of the audience could not bear the burden of fare. They seemed to be weary of the playacting and soon got unenthusiastic. Girish Ghosh's death marked the decline of a long marvellous chapter in the history of Bengali theatre.

However, the plays of Sisir Bhaduri, a college lecturer of English, contributed a lot to the growth and development of theatre in the period of crisis. He devoted himself to the cause of restoring Bengali theatre its former glory by giving up his job and becoming a full time professional artist. Very soon by 1925, he had acquired an acclaim as a naturalistic actor and director from the learned and elite, and an amazing praise from public and press. Due to his inspiration, a host of realistic performers, like Ahindra Choudhury, Nirmalendu Lahiri, Naresh Mitra, Durgadas Banerjee, and Sarajubala Devi made their mark on the changed perceptions of the playgoers. "But by the mid-1930s,...theatre had once again entered the doldrums. Despite the debut of many excellent actors and actresses, drama seemed oblivious to the reality of changing socio-economic and historical conditions. The rise of cinema resulted in the defection of talent from theatre." (Lal 13)

Situation again was managed when the Bengali unit of the Indian People's Theatre Association (IPTA) impressively organized the performance of *Nabanna* (New Harvest) by Bijon Bhattacharya in 1944. It proved to be a land-marking play which created a sensation in the Bengali theatrical world. It was enthusiastically received in Calcutta and elsewhere. But the prestige remained short-lived. The main reason was the lack of unity. Many members left and formed troupes of their own, which generated the 'new drama movement'. This remained a minority phenomenon for many years but steadily acquired leadership of Bengali theatre.

The focus of the new movement was the depiction of the lives of the exploited and downtrodden people. Bengali theatre, now onwards, committed itself to the cause of presenting the socio-politico-cultural issues. Various groups came into existence from 1940s to 1960s. With the encouragement of Manoranjan Bhattacharya and Sombhu Mitra, a group called Bohurupee built its foundation in 1948 firmly enough for it to be active even now. Very soon, it acquired a prominent status for having touched sensitive contemporary issues in bold and effective manner. "Mitra was without question the supreme actor-director of contemporary Bengali theatre. Of Bohurupee's many achievements under his lead, the most exciting were the magnificent productions of several of Rabindranath Tagore's major plays, considered till then unstageable" (Lal 14). The group also had actors of high calibre, including Gangapada Basu, Amar Ganguli, Tripti Mitra, Kumar Roy, Sabitabrata Dutta, Khaled Choudhary and the lighting designer Tapas Sen.

Utpal Dutt, with his Marxist beliefs, formed the Little Theatre Group (LTG). The revolutionary plays were staged one after another at the old playhouse Minerva that was taken on lease for nearly ten years. These performances revealed Dutt's exceptional talent as actor, director, and dramatist. Under his inspiring leadership, the others also performed a remarkable role in this theatrical movement. Notable among them were Shekhar Chatterjee, Satya Bandopadhyay and his own wife Sova Sen, a gifted and versatile actress with an uncommon managerial ability, whose boundless capacity for work contributed tremendously to the success that the group achieved.

Nandikar, a theatre group established in 1960, stood out into an advantageous position with its adaption of Pirandello's

Six Characters in Search of an Author. It won high acclaim for the excellence of its productions and the performances of its members, especially those of the remarkable actress Keya Chakrabarti and actor Rudraprasad Sengupta. The group's early productions were mainly adaptations of non-Indian plays. Notable and the unforgettable works in this period included the adaptations of Chekhov's *Cherry Orchard* and Pirandello's *Henry IV* as well as the translation of Anouilh's *Antigone.* In 1969, Nandikar took on lease a new playhouse, named Rangana, where the adaptations of Brecht's *Three Penny Opera* and *Good Person of Setzun* drew large crowds. Chakrabarti's untimely death and Bandyopadhyay's departure did not hamper its popularity. It continued to stage a variety of plays under Sengupta's stewardship. At the same, it hosted a prestigious annual national theatre festival. In the later period, no group relied more on foreign drama for material.

In 1966, Bibhash Chakraborty, as the director and leading personality, had organised Theatre workshop. It proved to be a distinguishing event due to its policy of giving introduction to the works of the new dramatists. The group theatres presented plays mostly at the newly built Academy of Fine Arts. In 1960, Souvanik built Mukta Angan. It contributed significantly to the development of the Bengali theatre with the staging of the experimental plays as well as by renting out Mukta Angan at affordable rates. Notable instance was the premiering show of the epoch-making play *Evam Indrajit* by Badal Sircar. Another unique group named Theatre Centre was formed in 1954 by Tarun Roy.

Sircar continued writing equally powerful plays after *Evam Indrajit* and came to be recognized as one of the foremost playwrights of Indian theatre. Very soon, he won an international recognition with the establishment of a new form of theatre to which he called Third Theatre. Many of his disciples took this movement outside Kolkata, while a few used it to extend the development of theatre within Kolkata.

A decentralization of proscenium group theatre into district towns resulted in creating a flourishing theatre culture in places like Kalyani and Baharampur and it remained inspiring and helpful to the development of theatrical activities. Other eminent authors in this period were Manoj Mitra, Mohit Chattopadhyaya, Dwijen Bandyopadhyay and Debasis Majumdar. Although substantial original playwriting continued to appear, the lack of superior literary and theatrical craftsmanship often remained an anxiety. Periodically, critics also complained about the dependence of Bengali drama on the foreign drama.

In the last decade of the twentieth century, the new drama movement's passion disappeared and Bengali theatre again received a set-back. The main reasons of it were the violent political turbulence in West Bengal, and the introduction of video and television. Theatre could not attract spectators in the crowd it had been accustomed to. Nevertheless, it remained vibrant, with possibly the largest number of active troupes and new productions.

At the turn of the century, women troupes, with their gender issues, accorded a lot to theatre. To mention a few of them were Sima Mukhopadhyay, a dramatist, director and actress, Saoli Mitra, daughter of Sombhu and Tripti Mitra and Sohag Sen, a leading personality in giving new directions in a spectrum of forms and styles. Younger men followed in her footsteps to ensure for themselves greater freedom of performance. The most consistent and prolific theatre personality of this generation was Bratya Basu, an actor, director, and writer with highly unorthodox and radical thoughts.

Finally, to sum up, it can be stated that one has to pay a careful attention to the increasing activity in children's theatre and theatre in educational field. The major groups like Nandikar and others, too, have given encouragement to the activity of outreaching the projects at school and college level and also at the underprivileged sections who, with a proper training, can offer a hopeful future to theatre.

The First Phase of Bengali Theatre: Utpal Dutt

Like most theatre workers of the period, Utpal Dutt too was moved to join the IPTA at its beginning. However, he left it within ten months and started the People's Little Theatre in 1947. Though the association existed for a very short period, the format of the IPTA ballets worked on his artistic approach. It is for this reason that his theatre, in its initial phase, can be considered as an extension of the experiments made by the IPTA. But very soon, in the seventies, he reverts once again to his old picture frame productions. With the very effective use of the folk form Jatra, he has tried to discuss the current socio-political issues. Kironmoy Raha opined: "Dutt is commonly taken to represent the "radicalisation of political thinking in Bengal in the post-independence period" and one who actually gave the political theatre a "left-ideological colouration." (Raha 134)

Though Dutt has formally started his theatrical career in 1947, it was only after securing the lease of the Minerva theatre in 1959 that he could create his identity and acquire a position as one of the leading playwrights of Bengali theatre. Among the early Minerva plays, *Angar, Kallol,* and *Ferari Faul* are notable. "At this stage, Dutt saw his commitment in terms of "the message" that the art work was expected to propagate and set out to pursue his goal in work after work" (Chukerbutty 39). All the early plays became quite popular among the public. However, as pointed out by Barthes, theatre is rendered into "an extremely dense semantic act" a form of "informational polyphony" (Barthes 262) made up of six or seven items of information comprising the set, the costumes, the lighting, the placing of the actors, their gestures, and their speech.

The effective use of light is a central part in Dutt's theatre. Following in the footsteps of Tapas Sen, the veteran playwright, he too uses the principle of reflected light and tries to present a three-dimensional effect on the stage, that is, the use of transparent lighting in which the illumination comes wholly or partly through a semi-transparent backdrop and the backdrop gives a sense of 'livingness' to the background. His first play *Angar* which deals with the incident of the drowning miners has created a sensation in the theatrical world. Dutt, here, in collaboration with Tapas Sen has continued to use light to deepen the sense of magical charm. The same strain is resumed in the production of *Stalin 1934* that opened at the theatre in February 1980. The light effects are used to intensify the emotional impact of the death of Stalina. Her suicide was heightened with the lights dimming onstage and the transparent backdrop in which Stalina's action of stabbing herself to death was mimed through a figure of shadow. The music accompanied remained helpful in increasing the intensity of the pathetic impact. The sensationalism created by the death of Stalina symbolizes the horrible nature of Stalin's dictatorship in Russia under the name of Marxism.

Dutt, in his theatre followed the track of naturalism and the folk form Jatra, however, with some changes as per the demand of his work. In the use of naturalistic set, he summons up a world of objects. This is related to the belief that "reality is an ensemble of visible and calculable commodities" (Suvin 74) as against a mere dynamic approach to reality that develops during the second phase of this theatre. In *Stalin 1934*, the stage was a place of hotchpotch, full of a phone-board, chairs, tables, sofas, the piano, etc.: the whole place had been utilised to accommodate the furniture; every detail had been worked out; the aim was to present authentically the immediate scene: Russia in the 1930s. The meticulous authenticity of detail which is the characteristic quality of Utpal Dutt's plays is something that is expected, demanded and enjoyed by the contemporary Calcutta audience. For example, in *Stalin 1934,* the cluttering of the objects on the stage creates an oppressive space which is the main focus of the play. Dutt has used objects to provide a backing to the visual.

Coupled with Dutt's illusionism is his use of the costume that aims at evoking a sense of historical truth. The good costume is meant to be merely a sign which signifies the character's social and emotional condition. Pronoti Chukerbutty is of the opinion that Dutt, in the use of costume, highlights the vestimentary details more like a painter obsessed with pictorial authenticity. This deteriorated principle of imitation makes Dutt's theatre fall in line with the bourgeois theatre, that is, theatre which aims to appeal and entertain the general audience, in spite of its explicitly formulated socialist message. (Chukerbutty 45)

Utpal Dutt's plays inherited the Scribean characteristics. Eugene Scribe was interested in holding the concentration of the audience by using the attention-calling devices. For this, he devised a theatrical formula known as *la piece bien faite* or "the well-made play". It is a play with a complicated and highly artificial plotting, a rise of suspense, a scene of climax in which all problems and mysteries are resolved, and a happy ending. The subject-matters of such plays are the traditional romantic conflicts, misunderstandings between characters, mistaken identities, secret information, lost or stolen documents, and similar devices led to the formation of suspense. The plot is usually based on a secret known to the audience and withheld from the major characters so as to be revealed to them in a climactic scene. A part of the plot is based on some misunderstanding with entrances, exits, letters, revelations of identities and other similar devices used to heighten the suspense. Dutt too uses such strategies in his plays, which are full of intrigue and suspense.

Scribe's plays often dealt with the depiction of the good and bad fortunes experienced by the hero which ultimately resulted in highlighting the emotional rhythm. He made his plays 'topical' and up-to-date because that used to act in harmony of the taste of a middle-class audience. It is noticed that most of the important plays of Dutt have 'topical' themes related to the contemporary sensitive issues. The notable examples are Vietnam War (*Ajeya Vietnam*), the Black Question (*Manusher Adhikarey*), the Naxalite Problem (*Teer*), etc.

The structure of the well-made play has a firm grip on the psyche of the audience and it ultimately results in receiving their comfortable contemplation. But being superficial in structure and nature, it lacks the capacity of disturbing or challenging the pre-suppositions of the audience as demonstrated by Brecht in the *Three Penny Opera*.

It is noticed that Utpal Dutt's theatre is also embedded in the Aristotlian tradition. With its sensational appeal, bewitching well-made structure, and the pathetic end, the play appeals to passion rather than to reason. *Angar* dealing with the sufferings of the miners is ended with a spectacle of the enmeshed miners slowly engulfed and drowned by the rising waters of the mine. *Kallol*, based on the naval mutiny in Bombay, in 1946, is concluded with a magnificent scene of the hero in the midst of the roaring of the guns, and seemed to be outwitting the situation but suddenly getting killed. *Ferari Fauj*, based on the terrorist activities in Bengal in the pre-independence era also came to an end with the death of the hero Ashok. Thus, it is noticed that Dutt employs the tragic mode to project the revolutionary consciousness. So, the ending of the play appears to be totally contradictory to the expectation of the playwright. Instead of arousing the sense of revolution, the play creates the feeling of pity.

In most of his plays such as *Angar, Ferari Fauj, Barricade,* and *Kallol,* Dutt employs the form of Aristotelian tragedy, which depicts the shift from pleasure to calamity and naturally is puzzled and confused at what results. Identifying the anti-revolutionist effect of these plays, he himself proclaims later: "I think, I was politically confused myself at the time. At that time, I had thought the play *Angar* ending with a revolutionary stuff. It seemed quite enough in terms of the political parties. But when I looked back in 1964, I found *Angar*, utterly worthless. I had been telling people, "Look at those hapless ones drowning, and pity them." (Dutt Interview with Bandyopadhyay n.p.)

It should also be noted that in his search for a true revolutionary idiom Dutt was one of the pioneers in introducing street theatre and poster plays into realm of radical theatre in Bengal (Chukerbutty 55). In his *Manusher Adhikarey,* he succeeds in matching a revolutionary content to revolutionary form. The development and perfection of handling displayed by Dutt in this play makes it remarkable. And in the course of time, it came to be recognized as his masterpiece.

In her contemplation on Utpal Dutt's contribution, Pronoti Chukerbutty remarks: "In its journey towards a more careful realism, the Bengali theatre had touched its first port of call in the theatre of Utpal Dutt but the vast ocean was still beckoning unchallenged and Badal Sircar was to appear on the horizon with the promise of a new fulfilment." (Chukerbutty 60)

The Second Phase: Realism in Bengali Theatre

A remarkable change is noticed in modern Bengali theatre towards the beginning of the twentieth century. The theatre aims at establishing a socialist society. Right from the beginning it has been influenced by the European theatre. Therefore, it is necessary to study its development in connection with the later one. The development of theatre can be categorised into two phases: the pre-Brechtian or the content-oriented phase and more formally self-conscious, the Brechtian phase. The first one is typified by the theatre of Utpal Dutt in Bengal and Arnold Wesker in Britain while, the second one is represented by the theatre of Badal Sircar in Bengal and Edward Bond in Britain.

After the mid-century, alternative theatre, more particularly, left-wing theatre had achieved prominence both in Britain and Calcutta. The first phase of this theatre was marked by an overemphasis of the new content to gain a 'reality effect'. This phase had its roots in the theoretical position that considered the representation of historical reality as its sole aim and purpose. This involvement with the new content was a characteristic feature common to the first phase of the Left-wing theatre. It had begun with the early Indian People's Theatre Association days and continued up to the theatre of Utpal Dutt.

Instead of presenting sentimental love-scenes, the playwrights in the twentieth century successfully tried to hold a faithful mirror of life in their plays. Actually, long ago, the movement towards photographic realism started in the European theatre with Victor Hugo in 1830. It was followed by the plays of Emile Zola, Henric Ibsen, George Bernard Shaw, Strindberg, etc. Utpal Dutt was one of the earliest Indian playwrights to turn to this nineteenth century European tradition and to accept the naturalistic style of production in his plays. Naturalism had a profound impact on the production techniques of theatre in this period.

The focus of this Left-wing theatre was on individual development; the cross-section of human life was presented psychologically. Instead of the hero, heroine and villain, the farmers and the working class people became the characters of the plays of this period. However, the actions of the main characters were guided by their own subjective passions or by the rhetoric of heart. Action in this phase was then subjectively directed and not shown to be the result of objective circumstances.

Although got influenced by naturalism, the Left-wing theatre, in its preliminary phase, also was embedded in the Aristotlian tradition of tragedy aimed at evoking catharsis, a form of purification, a correction of the passion that used to create disorder in society. By the terrifying spectacle of the catastrophe, the playwright tried to cure the spectator of his disorderly trait. Due to its purpose of restoring repose and balance, Aristotlian tragedy failed to become a model for the creation of revolutionary tendencies within the audience. On the contrary, it created counter-revolutionary effects. In the later period, Bertolt Brecht replaced Aristotlian empathy with the estrangement effect in the theatre. This insight was not operational during the early phase of the Left-wing theatre.

The Left-wing theatre, in its second phase, created a new self-consciousness. Representation of reality was its sole aim and the experiments of Bertolt Brecht were at the pivot of the development. Brecht had shown that through the 'distancing' of experience on the stage it was possible to extract an accurate meaning from it. For him, the meaning arises in the consciousness of the spectator not through empathy and illusionism but logically through an appeal to his rationality. Thus, theatre, in its second phase, was to experiment with non-representational modes to achieve a representational effect.

In Brechtian theatre, the theatrical image has a functional role. It is not used to double or to make gaudy the already given image of the world. Rather, it is used as a mode of signification—a medium of meaning making. "In Sircar's theatre, the powerful presentation helps to reconstitute the perception of the audience making them more aware and responsive.... It leaves a powerful impression, nevertheless, helping the audience to achieve a comprehensive view of existing reality" (Chukerbutty 11). For Sircar, rapt attention is also a form of participation. Therefore, he forced the audience not to anticipate but to watch the play with careful attention to apprehend the reality properly. Naturally, there is a consolidation of a new self-consciousness.

The playwrights of this period have discovered that the interaction of living organism is the greatest strength of theatre. It is a live communication between a group of human beings physically present in a particular time and place. The performers interact among themselves and also with the spectators. Another noteworthy change is the rejection of the stage-auditorium dichotomy that led to open out an infinite variety of possibilities in the theatre. The ultimate upshot of this is the development of the concept of the environmental theatre. Sircar has demanded the participation of the audience into the action of the play. For him, the spectator is not an object to be acted upon but a subject enacting a role through his very positioning within the theatrical space. Sircar says: "The language of this theatre involves being within and experiencing not viewing and hearing from a separate sanctum at a distance. It involves projecting individually at another human being and receiving feedback from his response, here and now." (Sircar, *Enact*; qtd. in Pronoti 13)

Utpal Dutt and Arnold Wesker have used theatre to propagate and to instruct by adding arguments and discussions into the body of the play. But the second wave playwrights like Sircar and Bond let the meaning arise from juxtaposing the situations. Sircar goes a step ahead by making his theatre open ended and thereby, leaving the actors and spectators to cope with the action and to ponder over the situation projected in the play.

The two phases described so far co-relate closely with developments within Marxist Aesthetics. It is a well-known fact that Marx did not leave behind well defined Marxist aesthetics. However, due to the persistence of literary critics like Georg Lukacs, we have today a well formulated, systematized basis for evaluating realistic art. The first historical evidence of the manifestation of the new socialistic consciousness in aesthetics is to be seen in the literature of Socialist Realism in the Soviet Union in the early thirties, but that is with the disastrous results.

Sircar is totally opposed to the naturalistic representation that has been loosely termed 'realism' in the theatre. Both Badal Sircar and Edward Bond have rejected the representational realism in the theatre. Sircar says: "In the name of creating an 'illusion of reality' naturalistic plays have been written and realistic sets have been created," (Sircar, *Third* 17) but in the theatre, spectators are ready to use their imagination and the attempt of the "theatre-realist to delude them" (Sircar, *Third* 19) is both unfruitful and redundant. Edward Bond has rejected the scenic stage for the bare stage with minimum functional props.

The rejection of the scenic stage is also partly due to the influence of Bertolt Brecht. Edward Bond openly admits his adherence to the Brechtian tradition recognizing at the same time the need to move ahead. (Bond 34)

Sircar's theatrical art is also reminiscent of that of Brecht's art, that is, his Epic Theatre which has opened out new possibilities for a committed approach to art. Thus, the Brechtian aesthetics has provided a progressive model for the second phase of the Left-wing theatre. However, an attempt has been made to transcend Brecht and efforts in this direction have been made by Badal Sircar.

Badal Sircar: A Brief Biographical Sketch

Born in 1925, in a middle-class Bengali family, Badal Sircar took his degree of civil engineering in 1947. While working as an engineer in Maithon, a distant town from Calcutta, he established a 'rehearsal club' out of his keen interest in theatre since his childhood. However, disheartened with the available plays, he himself started writing plays. Between 1956 and 1964, Sircar came out with six comedies: *Solution X, Baropisima, Sanibar, Ram Shyam Jadu, Ballabhpurer Rupakatha, and Kabikahini*. But it was with *Evam Indrajit* (1963) he came to be recognized as one of the major Indian playwrights. The play attracted wide attention and acclaim for its striking originality.

Sircar worked as the civil engineer in India for eleven years before moving to England in 1957 where he worked and studied for two years. Again in 1963, he visited France with a scholarship to study town planning. After staying in Calcutta for a brief period, Sircar went to Nigeria in 1964. It was while working there that he wrote quite a few major proscenium plays such as *Baki Itihas* (That Other History), *Tringsha Shatabdi* (The Thirtieth Century), and *Pagla Ghoda* (The Crazy Horse). He returned to Calcutta in 1967. Before devoting his life fully to theatre, he had been abroad twice: first, on a tour of the East European countries in 1969 on a cultural exchange programme and second, to the USA in 1972 with a Jawaharlal Nehru Research Fellowship. This time, he met a few avant-garde practitioners like Rechard Schechner and Julian Beck who were to influence him to a certain extent.

After his return from Nigeria, in 1967, Sircar established his theatre group "Satabdi". Initially "Satabdi" would perform both on and off proscenium. But under Sircar's leadership, not only did "Satabdi" reject the proscenium, but it also dispensed with such artificial aids as elaborate costumes, props, make-up, lights, and sounds. "In order to meet the demands made by the new thrust in his theatre, Sircar started writing a new set of plays. The three plays *Procession, Bhoma*, and *Stale News* belong to this phase of playwriting." (Dutta 5)

Sircar wrote, acted in, directed and produced some of the most influential and progressive plays of post-independence India. A pioneer of the People's Theatre movement in India—'Third Theatre'—Sircar had worked as the social reformer to make people aware of their responsibilities in fighting an unjust system and to change their mind-set.

Sircar was of the opinion that it was not human beings but society that needed to be reformed first. The five proscenium plays that he wrote between 1963 to 1970, *Evam Indrajit, Baki Itihas, Tringsha Shatabdi, Sarkas*, and *Shesh Nei*—exhibit Sircar's refusal to accept society as it is and his desperate search for the right path to follow.

Sircar is widely known for his new brand of theatre. A pioneer of the experimental theatre in Kolkata, he is well-known as a famous playwright, actor, and director. His works, originally written in Bengali, have been translated into several Indian languages. He has been honoured with the Padma Shri, the Sangeet Natak Akademi Award, Kalidas Samman, Jawaharlal Nehru Fellowship, and the Sangeet Natak Akademi Fellowship.

Badal Sircar's Contribution to the Indian Theatre

Badal Sircar, an avant-garde playwright of the second phase of Left-wing theatre, has liberated the Bengali stage from its servile imitation of the Victorian theatre of Britain. It is observed that in the first phase of the realistic theatre in Bengal, there was the tendency of ignoring both form and phrasing. In Utpal Dutt's theatre, political militancy overpowers literary technique. He himself clarifies his role stating: "The audience is our first concern; matters of form and content come second." (Dutt, Gunawardana 225)

Sircar, with his radical theatre, has successfully established a co-ordinate relation between political tendency and literary technique. It is with him that experimentation was given a workable position in Bengali Theatre. His dramaturgy marks a sharp break with that of Utpal Dutt's who in his attempt to attract the audience, has led to the formation of a theatre obviously consumerist in outlook. With the introduction of his "poor theatre", Sircar rejects the consumerism and liberates the theatre from maintaining a buyer-seller relationship with the spectator. Sircar's theatre is a free theatre. According to him, "Theatre is a human act, hence, all human beings involved, whether as performers or as spectators, should be free in their relationship with one another, and no external factor should affect that relationship." (Sircar, *Third* 76)

In his dramatic art, Sircar, like Brecht, also has rejected the naturalism of the scenic stage and illusionism created by the interplay of light, and costume. It is with him that the analytical approach to dramatic technique is incorporated in Bengali theatre which made him to give up the Bengali popular folk form Jatra which was deeply entrenched in the mythico-religious tradition and therefore, quite naturally, could not help being rendered into a sentimental melodramatic form. "Apart from a critical approach to theatrical form and structure, the Left-wing theatre in its second phase was to have a more complex philosophical basis" (Chukerbutty 67). Actually, it gets influenced by the diverse literary transitions in Europe.

With the publication of *Critique of Dialectical Reason,* Sartre attempted to synthesize Existentialism and Marxism, the two dominant trends of the twentieth century. The book displayed the various positions Sartre had taken in his literary voyage. Initially, he was dissatisfied with the dogmatic Marxists, since he was the staunch advocate of the thought that man was the master of his own destiny. But in existentialism, as Lukacs noted, the individual did not possess the power to influence others and the power to shape history. So, there was no inter-subjectivity of social relation in Sartre's existentialism. However, with the publication of his *Critique of Dialectical Reason,* Sartre showed his first philosophical siding with Marxism and his "Existential Marxism opened out a new direction in European thought attempting to overcome in the process, strict philosophical isolation." (Chukerbutty 69)

Badal Sircar's Third Theatre is born out of this synthesis of the dual tradition of Existentialism and Marxism. Sircar, right from the beginning, has been in the search of such form of theatre that would comprise his avant-garde experiments, his earlier vision of an individualised subjectivity for a Brechtian form of theatre and his contemplation of making it people's theatre. His theatre aims at redirecting the theatrical experience according to the developments in European thought, to retain the freedom of tone as well as to rouse it from its apathy with regard to form. Therefore, one can notice that his theatre sets out to achieve the fusion of the various traditions in Europe. In this sense, he fulfils Barthes expectations about the playwrights where the later says: "We are entitled to expect a great deal from a playwright who might give the new political art the de-conditioning powers of the old avant-garde theatre." (Barthes 70; qtd. in Pronoti 70)

Sircar's early plays such as *Evam Indrajit, Baki Itihas, Tringsha Shatabdi* and *Pagla Ghoda* display his exceptional strength as an avant-garde playwright. The plays explore man's consciousness towards his existential responsibilities, his profound sense of guilt for turning away from them and leading an alienated life. Sircar thinks that the social relevance of a play, for a sincere writer, is quite automatic. However, this attitude has to be replaced by a more insightful one at a later phase when Sircar looks upon the work of art as a means of reaffirming natural justice in a society burdened with man-made laws (Chukerbutty 71). In the plays of this phase, Sircar has utilised the modern techniques such as simultaneity, montage and multi-focus to forge a contemporary artistic medium. This attempt helps him to mark a sharp break with the contemporary Bengali theatre that is obsessed with the style of presentation prevalent in the Victorian theatre of England and to raise it to a new height of artistry unknown to it.

In *Evam Indrajit* Sircar successfully tried to give the banality of everyday life a dramatic garb. The exploration of the theatrical quality of everyday life, the assigning of different roles to the same character were new experiences for the Indian theatre which often dealt with traditional characterization. According to Pronoti Chukerbutty, "On the philosophical plane the play, dealing with the alienated consciousness of modern man, showed Sircar's awareness of the problem arising from the recentering of knowledge from its Divine locus to a human centre that was responsible for the crisis in the modern world" (Chukerbutty 74-75). The play left the audience disturbed and spell-bound with its central issue: that the problem in the contemporary life is not to live or to die but to endure. That is why the play has ended with a message that to be among the living is to be living.

The experiences narrated in the plays of the pre-realistic avant-garde phase such as *Evam Indrajit, Baki Itihas, Shesh Nei, Pagla Ghoda, Sari Raat* tend to be static. They display Sircar's conscious and critical attitude that is at the same time dogged by dumbness, a negation, an acceptance of the despair of modern existence. The plays in the second phase deal with the existential issues such as: an individual feeling unexpectedly "thrown" into the world, the sense of isolation, insufficiency and impotence inherent in the human condition with the resultant sense of despair and anguish. The meaninglessness or absurdity of existence echoed vigorously through these plays is actually a central creed of existentialism that is postulated on the level of philosophy by Heidegger, Sartre and Camus.

In the early phase, Sircar's men are more passive than active, to be acted upon more than capable of acting for themselves, lacking in bold aggressiveness, their anger and frustration become their only positive statements. However, in the later phase of his evolution, Sircar has successfully transcended this merely critical approach. In this later phase, he represents the individual as a member of a society, a social force constantly engaged in transforming reality.

Transition in Sircar's Theatre

Sircar's theatre is the theatre of protest. It shows his shift from anger to commitment. However, the form of protest in the realistic phase is distinct from that of in the pre-realist phase. In this second phase, Sircar could turn away from the purely ethical protest to a theatre that would look after not a sense of man's discomfort and nausea in his struggle for existence but would attack the real, that is, the political structure of society.

The social situation in Bengal remains responsible for this transition in Sircar's career as a playwright. The turmoil in the political life in the sixties challenged the established and accepted social values rendering them into pieces. The inhuman killing, violence and massacre of the emerging youthful militancy in the Naxalite Movement left the older generation probing, disturbed, helpless, confused and introspective. The pressing reality of the day was the changing political situation and the theatre could not afford to turn a deaf ear to it. Sircar himself stated, "In the early sixties, a rapid change was noticed in the theatre scene. A number of 'Group Theatres' developed, who rejected the old fashioned stereo-typed plays and tried to say something that had some bearing with contemporary life.... This was the situation when I established 'Shatabdi' in 1967." (Sircar, *Third* 10-11)

The political upheaval in the society rendered Sircar to rethink on the role that a theatre can perform in changing the mind-set of people. He was convinced that art had a definite role to play in the transformation of society and though it might not be able the sole means in bringing about this social change, it had an important part to play in it. To quote Sircar's words: "The dichotomy in the cultural field cannot be removed without a fundamental change in the socio-economic situation and I have no illusion that it can be done simply through theatre. But I do believe that theatre can be one of the many facets of a movement that is vitally needed to bring about the desirable change...." (Sircar, *Third* 3)

Sircar's experiences in the avant-garde theatre remain supportive to his involvement with the realistic stage since the basis of many of the innovations in it was his acute observation of life. The establishment of 'Shatabdi' in 1969, also helped to strengthen his resolution to "re-conceive the very materiality of the theatre and not merely its political ideology." (Barthes 70; qtd. in Pronoti 83-84)

Sircar knew that the two were closely intertwined and a limited set of theatrical conventions was inadequate to express reality which was in the state of constant flux. Contemporaneity in theme became the hallmark of this theatre which added richness to it. It was a theatre which relied on the complex relationship of the artist to the spectator, the spectator to the performance, and the performer to the spectator making the theatrical experience a live medium of communication.

Sircar, here, gave up his earlier stance of representing reality in the static manner. Being a man of science field, Sircar could read the changed relation between man and nature affected by science. He was also aware of the fact that feedback, that is, spectator's response to the performance acquired a unique position in theatrical art. So, he used theatre as a means not to provide an entertainment but to raise a question about the basic complacency of the audience and thus, leave them disturbed by imparting a new awareness.

To make theatre people's theatre, Sircar decided to utilize Grotowski's concept of poor theatre in the true sense of that term. So, he reduced the use of sets, lights, costumes, background music, and mechanical devices. He himself stated: "We adopted the concept of poor theatre in the literal sense, that is, inexpensive theatre. Our group was poor, so are our countrymen but we wanted to utilise poverty and turn it into an advantage instead of a restriction." (Sircar, *Third* 41)

The rejection of the stage-auditorium technique helped Sircar to develop successfully in India Richard Schechner's concept of an "Environmental space theatre". However, he went a step ahead since, like Schechner, he did not look upon theatre just as a "visual-verbal participatory game" that can enhance the entertainment. Instead, theatre, for him, was backed by a seriousness of purpose. In this new form of theatre, space was used to develop an actor-spectator intimacy in an atmosphere of understanding and physical closeness. The spectator became a part of the architecture of action. This closeness enabled Sircar to achieve a firm grip on the psyche of the audience and to have a desired effect. In his theatre, the performer created within the spectator a feeling of community, that is, a sense of "we" against "them" of the establishment. Through the numerous workshops, held periodically all over the country, Sircar, remained successful in creating a liberated spectator capable of launching into the action.

While developing the new stage techniques, Sircar was alert of the possibility of the fact that "where the illusion of character is too opaque, the humanity of the performer gets submerged beneath the role. The actor's role transfers to him an aura that differentiates him qualitatively from the spectator and destroys the sense of rapport. It was for this purpose that Brecht insisted on the performer being the demonstrator of the role rather than the enactor of it..." (Chukerbutty 93). It is for this reason that Sircar insisted on maintaining the distance on the part of both: the actor and the spectator. Like Brecht's Epic Theatre, his play expected the participation of the audience into the action of the play with an emotional detachment.

Sircar also changed the relationship of the text to the theatrical performance. He aimed at creating a play prepared by a group, a collective action rather than an individual one. In majority of the plays of this phase, no script was used at all. The performance involved for the most part conversation with the spectators. Similarly, in some of his plays, Sircar prepared the text with the clippings of political, economic, and sentimental news, with newspaper photographs. In making of the text of the play *Stale News*, this technique was employed and what ultimately emerged from the collaging together of the group experience centered round the problem of the exploitation of the weak by the strong became the text of the play. With this, Sircar brought on the stage record of exploitation in the pre-

and post-independence Indian society and left the audience disturbed with the burning reality of the society claimed by Girish Karnad with reference to his play *Tale Danda*: "It seems 800 years have solved no problems. We are back exactly where we started." (Qtd. in Babu 50)

This new form also offered mobility to his theatre. He could put up inexpensive productions in slums, village greens, community halls, etc. This would help him to enlarge the audience and also thus, remould not only the city theatre but also to substitute the rural obsession with Jatra for a more up-to-date, non-sentimental form of theatrical experience.

Works Cited

Ali, Ahmed. "Progressive View of Art." *Marxist Cultural Movement in India: Chronicals and Documents* (1936-47), edited by Sudhi Pradhan, National Book Agency, 1979.

Babu, Manchi Sarat. "Social Deformity." *Indian Drama Today: Study in the Theme of Cultural Deformity.* Prestige, 1997.

Barthes, Roland. *Critical Essays.* Northwestern University Press, 1972.

Bond, Edward. "On Brecht: Letter to Peter Holland." *Theatre Quarterly*, III, No. 30 (Summer 1978).

Chukerbutty, Pronoti. *Phases in the Development of Realism in the Twentieth Century Drama: A Comparative Study of the Theatre in Bengal and Britain.* A dissertation submitted in partial fulfilment of the requirements for the degree of Master of Letters in English (English Literature). Central Institute of English and Foreign Languages (now, EFLU), 1982.

Dutta, Ella. Introduction. *Three Plays* by Badal Sircar, Seagull, 2009.

Dutt, Utpal. Interview with A.J. Gunawardana. *The Drama Review*, Vol. 15, No. 3 (Spring 1971).

———. Interview with Bandyopadhyay. No pagination.

Ghose, C.P. "Crisis in Bengal IPTA", quoted in Pronoti Chukerbutty.

Indian People's Theatre Association, No. 1, July 1943, rpt., edited by Sudhi Pradhan, *MCMI*.

Lal, Anand, editor. *Theatres of India: A Concise Companion.* OUP, 2009.

Pradhan, Sudhi, editor. "Manifesto: All India Progressive Writers Conference." *MCMI.* National Book Agency, 1979.

Raha, Kironmoy. *Bengali Theatre.* National Book Trust, 1978.

Sircar, Badal. *Enact* (March-April 1982), quoted in Pronoti Chukerbutty.

———. *On Theatre*. Seagull, 2009.

———. *The Third Theatre*. Aurobindo Press, 1978.

Suvin, Darko. "The Mirror and the Dynamo." *Radical Perspectives in the Arts*, edited by Lee Baxandall, Penguin, 1972.

The Early Phase: Proscenium Plays

3
Evam Indrajit: The Endless, Weary Way

Introduction

> Writing about Badal Sircar's *Evam Indrajit* is like going on a sentimental journey; a nostalgic foray into the recent past of the Indian theatre; an encounter with the bitter sweet memories of a struggling sensibility trying to strike roots in a barren land; because, after all, it is only in relation to Indian theatre history that *Evam Indrajit* really makes its presence felt. (Dubey i)

The play *Evam Indrajit* is a milestone in the history of modern Indian drama. Indrajit, the central character in the play, becomes the spokesman of the young generation of the 1960s since, in him, the contemporary youths discover all their aspirations, compromises as well as the sense of hopelessness and futility which ultimately result in the feeling of anguish and depression. Rustom Bharucha has linked this play to Beckett's *Waiting for Godot* (Bharucha 133). For Satyadev Dubey, *Evam Indrajit* is about the residue of the middle class, "Who have failed to adjust, align and ceased to aspire and also those who are enmeshed in the day-to-day struggle for survival." (Dubey ii)

Indrajit has withdrawn himself from the conventional society. He is angry, serious, frustrated, iconoclastic young man who represents the predicament of the middle class alienated man in an amoral, soulless society. The life portrayed here is absurd illogical, and irrational. The protagonist believes firmly that human life starts and ends in nothingness. So, he is confused with the questions: "Why should one carry on? What is there beyond the path?" The answer to these questions is given by the Writer who performs the role similar to that of a commentator.

> Walk on. Be on the road! We are the cursed spirits of Sisyphus. We have to push the rock to the top—even if it just rolls down. (59)

However, the more the Writer ties him (Indrajit) up in a plot with the chains of Acts, the more he escapes saying—"it isn't real". According to K. Venkata Reddy, "The play is a theatrically effective and crystallized projection of the prevalent attitudes, vague feelings and undefined frustrations, growing at the hearts of the educated urban middle class." (Reddy 58-59)

The Structure of the Play

The play starts with the Writer in the search of a theme to write a play. He is not able to write for the simple reason that he has 'nothing to write about'. However, Manasi encourages him to write a play. The Writer suddenly turns towards the audience and calls out to four late-comers and asks them to come on to the stage. As the four give their names as Amal, Vimal, Kamal and Nirmal, he does not accept the name of the fourth, Nirmal. So, he says: "No, it can't be. You must have another name." (4)

Nirmal ultimately confesses that he is actually Indrajit, the name of the mythical rebel, Meghnad, Ravana's son, who defeated Indra, the Indian Zeus. He called himself Nirmal because "he was scared of unrest, one invites unrest by breaking the norm" (5). "From this point in the play, the Writer takes over like a ubiquitous and omniscient presence, probing the lives of Amal, Vimal, Kamal, and Indrajit." (Dubey iii)

The play comprises three acts. They depict the three major phases of the lives of Amal, Vimal, and Kamal. The first act portrays their education, hobbies, pastimes and other things that characterize their college life. The second act describes their settlement with job and marriage. Their aspirations and/or ambitions get fulfilled in the third act: Amal gets a promotion as a manager in the ABC Company, Vimal buys a plot and builds a house there, and Kamal starts business to earn more money.

Indrajit is in love with Manasi and wants to marry her. But they cannot become the life-companion since she is his cousin on mother's side. He remains always conscious that he is Indrajit and different from his other companions. He wants to visit London for he believes that this visit will liberate him from the humdrum existence and banality of life. He is a rebel who wants to change the society drastically. Quite proudly, he tells Manasi: "If I hadn't tasted the fruit of knowledge, I could have gone on living in this paradise of your blessed society of rules. Now I can only batter my head against the wall" (23). To change his way of life, he goes on changing the places of his job from Calcutta to Bhopal, Bhopal to Bombay, Jullunder, Meerut and Udaypur. Manasi follows the taboo of society and does not accept his proposal for marriage. She settles in Calcutta as a school teacher. However, they are in touch with each other by writing letters and meeting once a year in Calcutta. He visits London but remains unsuccessful to change his life. After his return, he marries another Manasi and enjoys himself in his marital life. He becomes one of the middle-class men who are contended with their normal day-to-day life. He tells Manasi about his family: "My wife looks after the house. I work in the office. My wife goes to a film. I go with her. My wife goes to her parents' house. I eat in the restaurant; she comes back. I go marketing" (54). Quite unconsciously, he falls into the whirlwind of banal life that he has tried hard to shun. His marital life gives him a sad realization that he is not different from others. He illustrates his disillusionment to Manasi: "So long as I couldn't accept my ordinariness. I dreamt. Now I accept it.... Manasi don't call me Indrajit. I am Nirmal. Amal, Vimal, Kamal and Nirmal" (58-59). He calmly listens to the Writer's existential philosophy: "Walk. Be on the road! For us, there is only the road. We shall walk.... We are the cursed spirits of Sisyphus." (59)

The play *Evam Indrajit,* thus, conveys the central doctrine of existentialist philosophy: "Existence precedes essence" (Asolkar 18). K. Venkata Reddy, Veena Noble Dass and Eakambaram are all agreed in calling *Evam Indrajit* an absurd play. Eakambaram views it as an Indian version of *Waiting for Godot* (Babu 95). The character of Indrajit represents the angry young man belonging to the "lost generation" frustrated with the contemporary life and unable to do anything against its banality. The play ends with his realization that he is not different from others and life remains the same whether one is abroad or in India.

Critical Interpretation and Appraisal of the Play

The play *Evam Indrajit* centres round the eponymous character Indrajit. He refuses to accept society as it is and desperately tries to search the right path to follow. Amal, Vimal, Kamal, Nirmal and Indrajit are prototypical characters. The first four are delineated as caught in the web of meaningless, self-centered, and uneventful existence and, therefore, accept everything as it comes without raising a question. Indrajit is somewhat exceptional, since he wants to rebel against senseless obedience and conformity. But in his brave encounter with the bitter realities of life, he becomes exhausted and somewhat frustrated. "At the end of the play, however, he emerges as an undaunted individual. Unable to discover an ideological solution to the problems, Indrajit chooses the road rather than the destination." (Sarkar xv)

Indrajit is the representative of the urban middle-class that considers itself as the backbone of the country. The play makes these middle-class spectators introspective and renders them to feel guilty for opting for stability, aspiring for culture and believing in a national identity. The play is hailed as a 'mile stone' as it reflects a modern voice of protest, an anti-heroic mode, and a concern for realism that were all novel in the 1960s in Indian theatre.

Indrajit is unhappy, with the life around and is therefore, critical in his attitude towards life. He is reluctant to follow the norms of bourgeois culture. He wants to change the life but fails in his attempt. Feeling too much frustrated and dejected, he unsuccessfully attempts to commit suicide. This sense of self-destruction, of senseless wastage in the urban society, and a protest against it are the themes of the play.

The play is absurd in nature. K. Venkata Reddy states "...*Evam Indrajit*...was spontaneously received by the theatrical community in Bengal which discovered in the protagonist of the play, Indrajit, all their dreams and compromises and moments of hopelessness and futility. The play makes the point that "nothing worth mentioning ever happens," (41) the kind of feeling we get when we witness a typical 'absurd' play like... Beckett's *Waiting for Godot*." (Reddy 58)

The play-goers greet the play very profoundly, since it dramatizes the contemporary problems, they are facing—a significant social tension, the failure of man to solve his problems, his incapacity to adjust himself with the fast-changing materialistic society. In Indrajit's revolt against the norms of society, they have explored the realities of their circumstances. Satyadev Dubey rightly points out: The yearnings and dissatisfaction of an adolescent Indrajit or his insistence on an existence beyond geography are feelings that the educated middle-class mind has known often. His love for Manasi, the taboo attached to it, his wanting to break the taboo and failing to accomplish the tasks he sets before himself, his anger at the state of affairs and his total inability to do anything are again common experiences in India.... He finds our mean little world ridiculous.... Then comes a stage when he realizes that even the fulfilment of his love would not have provided the answer. A visit to London proves disappointing. He contemplates suicide as an act of faith, but finds himself incapable of the act. (Dubey iii-iv)

Indrajit's marriage with another Manasi indicates his adjustment and compromise with life. The earlier Manasi is still his friend. He narrates his marital life to her which is similar to the lives of the middle-class people in society. To quote Satyadev Dubey again:

> Indrajit finds himself at parallel railway tracks on either side-tracks with an illusory meeting point...the train does not come on these tracks any more.... He does not believe in his dreams any more, but he has now come to the bitter awareness that they were just dreams dreamt by a person who thought that he had the potential but in fact is a very ordinary person—he is Nirmal. (Dubey iv-v)

The Writer is persuaded by Manasi to write a play only about those who at that moment are sitting in the auditorium. However, he finds himself unable to write since he realizes that life is too chaotic and fragmentary to cohere into a dramatic mould and too mechanical to have any meaning. His agony is the agony of the artist who is deeply aware of the sterility and horror of life. "Badal Sircar, like T.S. Eliot in *The Waste Land,* offers no hope. The protagonist of the play ultimately meets with only despair, the key-note which is struck at the beginning itself." (Reddy 59)

In the initial stages, the Writer, actually grows hopeful of having found a hero for his play since Indrajit appears to him quite different from his fellow-companions Amal, Kamal and Vimal. He rejects to follow the beaten track of the middle-class people in society. The Writer conceives him to be a perfect protagonist of his play and sincerely strives to explore something meaningful in his life as it grows through his college days, his youthful love for a girl and his revolt against the whole set of social and moral convention. Amal, Vimal, and Kamal willingly become the cogs in the wheels and consequently, being with the current, flourish materially. Being different from them, Indrajit isolates himself from the norms of society and rejected the pleasures and happiness that the world offers him and further resists becoming a cog in the wheel as long as he can. But in his life, he cannot follow the dictum "rest not till the goal is achieved" and he cannot keep himself lingering behind, for he believes: "There is always a room on the top." In his desperate, frantic efforts to find meaning of existence he gets exhausted. Ultimately, he plods homewards his weary way since to toss from side to side on the sleepless bed, now becomes impossible for him. His failure in committing suicide makes him realize the harsh, undeniable reality of life: that being a tiny particle of this vast cosmos, he has to continue his painful journey on the endless road. He "is quick to see the Sisyphus analogy and the play ends with an assertion that goes beyond logic and reaches out to us like a cry for help from a drowning man with a sense of the essential and inescapable sadness of life" (Dubey v). Indrajit, like Beckett's Godot, "is an eternal question mark"

(Reddy 62). But Beckett ends his play at "waiting" while Sircar is determined to continue "searching".

The play is open-ended. The audience leaves the theatre not with a calm, pacified mind but with a disturbed mind. So, towards the end of the play is the beginning of the audience's consciousness. And continuation of the same theme is found in Sircar's succeeding play *Procession*. "Khoka is Indrajit's alter ego and the Old Man is almost a 'replica' of the 'Writer'. Indrajit and the Writer of *Evam* continue to be on the road even in *Procession*." Moreover, what the Writer says: "Its end is its beginning" (59), proves prophetic since its 'end' has found a new beginning for it in one of the subsequent plays *Procession*. (Bhattacharjee 126-27).

Similarly, it is observed that the characteristic attitude of Indrajit is found in majority of central characters in Sircar's plays. They appear to be caught in the web of enigmatic questions. They do not turn away from the problems. However, till the end, they remain undecided about the course of action they have to take. That is why Indrajit listens to the advice of the Writer to "be on the road"; Kumar of *Sarkas* finally concentrates on his research, and Sharad of *Baki Itihas* gives up his thought of committing suicide after hearing the news of his promotion to the post of an assistant professor.

The play *Evam Indrajit* resembles an absurd play even in its use of language. The dialogues in the play are repetitive and cynical. "Thus, the theme, the technique, and the language of *Evam Indrajit* link it with Absurd Drama.... The protagonist... searches for meaning in his life but finds, as in Sartre's *No Exit*, that there is no escape from ordinary life. Even when one is sincerely to be an Indrajit, one has got to end up as Nirmal.... It is not for nothing that it has been said that *Evam Indrajit* is *Waiting for Godot* in Indian Theatre." (Reddy 64)

Works Cited

Asolkar, Sharad. "Asitwawad ani Sartre." *Yugwani*, edited by Sharad Kolarkar, May 1980.

Babu, Manchi Sarat. "Physical Deformity." *Indian Drama Today: Study in the Theme of Cultural Deformity*. Prestige, 1997.

Bharucha, Rustom. *Rehearsals of Revolution: The Political Theatre of Bengal*. Seagull, 1983.

Bhattacharjee, Shampa. *Badal Sircar's Street Plays: A Thematic Study*. An M. Phil. Dissertation, submitted to Kakatiya University, Warangal, 1994.

Dubey, Satyadev. Introduction. *Three Modern Indian Plays*: *Tughlaq*, *Evam Indrajit*, *Silence! The Court is in Session*, translated by Girish Karnad and Priya Adarkar, OUP, 1989.

Reddy, K. Venkata. "Badal Sircar's *Evam Indrajit* as an Absurd Play." *New Directions in Indian Drama*, edited by Sudhakar Pandey and Freya Barua, Prestige, 1994.

Sarkar, Subhendu. Introduction. *Two Plays: Indian History Made Easy, Life of Bagala*, by Badal Sircar, OUP, 2010.

(N.B. All textual quotations are from *Three Modern Indian Plays*. OUP, 1989).

4

Baki Itihas: The Voice of Conscience

Introduction

The play *Baki Itihas* seems to be the sequel of the earlier play *Evam Indrajit* with the difference that Indrajit accepts the fallibility of existence while Sitanath demands responsibility on the part of the readers/audiences. Badal Sircar writes it in Nigeria in 1964-65. It is the seventh one in the series of his plays. The question raised by Indrajit: "What justifies middle-class man's existence?" becomes a lament of the protagonist of *Baki Itihas*. Anjum Katyal opines: "Like its predecessors *Ebong Indrajit* and *Sara Rattir*, it deals with the inadequacies and stultifying banality of a middle-class routine barricaded against the call of a larger life outside. What about the rest of history—the *baki itihas*—is the anguished cry that ends the play" (Katyal 60). So, here Sircar again exhumes and exposes the absurdity of the contemporary society and challenges the existence of man in the present war-ridden scenario. The play explores the guilt-consciousness of a middle-class man for being indifferent to the social condition and his responsibilities.

The Structure of the Play

The play has three acts. Sircar has written the third act first and "incorporated the first and second acts of the play to serve as a curtain raiser to the unexpected, shocking revelation of the history of oppression and cruelty" (Shodhganga 61). Sharad,

Vasanti and Sitanath are the main characters in the play and the other characters remain in the form of shadows used by the dramatist as per the necessity of situation.

The play starts with Vasanti reminding Sharad of the payment of electricity bill which he forgets to pay to the office as usual. Sharad is a professor and Vasanti is an aspiring writer. While overlooking the newspaper, they come across the news of suicidal death of Sitanath, a college professor, with whom they seem to have an acquaintance in past. Sharad asks Vasanti to write an imaginary story illustrating the anticipated causes of Sitanath's suicide.

In her story, Vasanti depicts Sitanath and Kanak leading a contented marital life. However, a summon from a court about the loss of the plot that Sitanath has purchased turns their family-life topsy-turvy. Sitanath succumbs to the blackmailing of Kanak's drunkard father whom she believes to be dead. Her father's constant threat that he will make Kanak a concubine renders Sitanath helpless and he goes on providing money to him for liquor which ultimately leads to bankruptcy. Having no alternative, he sells the land where Kanak has a dream of constructing their home. The bitter experiences in life such as the death of mother and elder sister due to poverty, another sister, leading the life of concubine leave Kanak totally insensible. Not knowing the true reason why her husband sold the land, she deserts him once and forever. Following the path of her sister, she declares to him that she is going to Nikhil, his friend, to lead a secure and stable life. The anguished words of her heart reflect her utter disillusionment with life: "There is nothing right, nothing proper in this world. No hopes, no dreams—only cold...." Having obsessed with the "maddening poverty", she fails to realise her sensible husband's feeling and Sitanath commits suicide having no reason to live life.

Sharad does not remain satisfied with Vasanti's story. So, he tries to interpret the cause of Sitanath's death through his story. The second act, which unfolds Sharad's version, is much more vague and complicated. It presents Sitanath as a vulture in the disguise of a man. Sharad describes him as suffering from "Lolita" complex. The story starts with Sitanath, the headmaster of the school, taking the decision to expel his student Ashok from school for reading Nabokov's novel *Lolita*. In spite of the request of Vidhi Babu, the Chairman of his school, he remains firm on his decision.

Actually, the novel *Lolita* reminds Sitanath the early days of his marital life when he and Kanak went to Chambalgad to spend their summer vacation. Parvati, a ten or eleven-year innocent, lovely daughter of Banwarilal used to stay with them. However, the slapping of Sitanath in a fit of anger renders Parvati run into the forest, where she falls a victim to the excessive physical lust of the dacoits. Sitanath, who goes in search of her, is found next day in wounded, unconscious situation in blood-stained tattered clothes. Imagining himself the dacoit, Sitanath thinks that his attraction for the little girl is the real cause of her tragedy. In spite of his conscious efforts, he cannot forget the incident and get himself relieved from that complex even after ten years. Narrating the incident to Vijay in the absence of his wife Kanak, he says: "Day and night that ugly, poisonous virus grew in my body.... Multiplying in thousands, millions, each moment."

The entry of Gauri, the ten year grand-daughter of Vidhi Babu intensifies his libido again. However, to avoid the future catastrophe, he commits suicide confessing: "I could not punish that devil for so long. But I will hang him today."

The story in third act hints at the true reason of Sitanath's suicide. The ghost of Sitanath appears in front of Sharad and gives him an album of pictures showing human cruelty and thirst for power. The album is actually the record of the history of violence, carnage, and bloodshed. It comprises the pictures of such incidents as Bhima drinking Dushasana's blood, slaves—naked and starved shackled in steel chains, Joan of Arc being burnt alive, and so on. Sitanath accuses Sharad of being unaware of the other side of history:

> Yes the rest of history. Which is not about examinations, not about jobs, not about marriage. Which is about oppression, violence, destruction, war, the suffering of centuries. The history of Pandav-Kauravs, Alexander,... Napoleon, Hitler. Thousands of years of history etched

> into the stones of the pyramids,...the walls of Jalianwala Bagh, the blasted earth of Hiroshima.

Sharad feebly tries to tell him, "There's another side to history. There's peace as well as war, love as well as oppression. It has to be." But his voice gets suppressed under the question of Sitanath: "Why didn't you end your life."

The play reaches to its climax in the third act. The real cause of Sitanath's suicide given by his own ghost is a heavy, astounding blow to the conscience of the readers. Actually, the ghost seems to the playwright's mouthpiece who questions the role of the middle-class man in the changing scenario which is characterised by unrest, genocide and bloodbath. He makes Sharad admit his guilt, that is, his indifference to the society around as well as his inability and helplessness to do anything to change this other side of history which comprises bloodshed, massacre of innocent people whose names are unknown to history.

Sitanath of the third version, the cause of whose suicide enthuses the playwright to write *Baki Itihas*, is the alter-ego of Sharad. It is his "private self". The reflection of his thinking is echoed in the conversation:

> Sharad: You can go now, Sharad.
>
> Sitanath: I am Sitanath.
>
> Sharad: You go Sitanath.

The conversation completes Sharad's identity with Sitanath.

Sitanath's question: "Why didn't you commit suicide, Sharad?" shakes his entire existence. It compels him to think over the cause of continued existence of middle-class man. Inability to find the answer makes Sharad restless. He is about to commit suicide but is interrupted by Vasudev, his friend, who brings the happy news of his promotion in job as an assistant professor. The play ends with Sharad returning to his routine, domestic life and Vasanti preparing and serving tea to them.

Critical Interpretation and Appraisal of the Play

Baki Itihas revolves round the three different versions of a story that have the same ending. The protagonist Sitanath and his wife Kanak appear in all the three versions while the other characters remain changing. Actually, the stories represent the different states of mind of a common man. A head line in a newspaper stimulates Sharad and his wife Vasanti, the intellectual members of the white-collar middle-class society to write a story. "What begins as an intellectual exercise soon morphs into a stifling commentary on mankind's selfish complacent existence and on his darkest thoughts—the kind that drives him to write those pages of human history that were best left unwritten!" (Shodhganga 56)

The play opens with the protagonist Sharad, a college professor and his wife Vasanti, a writer. They are thinking about their schedule on Sunday. A news item that describes the suicide of a person named Sitanath attracts their attention. Feeling that the dead person has a slightly known acquaintance, they try to guess the cause of his suicide. The analysis of Sitanath's death from three different dimensions forms the plot of the play. Vasanti thinks 'bankruptcy' and 'ruination' to be the causes of his suicide wherein the conflict arises due to the priority given to financial security by Sitanath's wife, Kanak who has hailed from a poverty-stricken home. She is incapable of distinguishing between the security offered by the material world and the sustained soul-stirring company offered by her husband. Sharad's anticipation about the same is quite shocking and complicated. In his story, he projects Sitanath suffering from 'Lolita fixation' a grown-up man having obsessed with a desire to have sex with an immature girl. The story ends with Sitanath committing suicide by strangling himself as a penance for his past deed and as a gesture of preventing its repetition in the future.

Sitanath's ghost is the protagonist of the third version of the story. His interpretation of man's history is a stunning revelation of the mystery to Sharad. This encounter reveals to Sharad the depressing and desolate side of the history of mankind referred to as "that remaining history" or "that other history". In his view, Sitanath enacts the role of the agent of an inhuman tradition. Contemplating in this vain, he begins to brood over the absurdity of his existence. The playwright here condemns the indifference of man, his alienation from the society which makes him blind to the predicament of his fellow-being in these so-called civilized third-world countries.

The play brings to notice a fact that material success and love of power lead man nowhere but towards wars and oppressions. "Power corrupts and absolute power corrupts absolutely." Innocent people become the victims of war due to their tendency of blindly following the orders of their master and also due to their incapacity to stop it. And the middle-class people like Sitanath, Sharad and Vasanti are either unaware of this other side of history or turn a deaf ear to it. While criticising the middle-class mentality, Anjum Katyal remarks, "This play intensifies the central concerns of *Ebong Indrajit* by asking the question—why should a middle-class subject not commit suicide? What justifies his continued existence? His modest, measured pleasures, the reassurance of his domestic routine, his steady rise through the ranks of his profession—are these enough to block out the violence and injustice that regains in that 'other' history?" (Katyal 61)

Antonin Artaud's Theatre of Cruelty aims to disturb the audience, to make them sensitive to the issues of life and to force them to realize the reality and to face it rather than to find the escape routes. According to him, "Art should not be a shadow of reality, but should strive as far as possible to be that reality itself to bring real passions and sufferings out of the shadows" (Shodhganga 58). The unveiling of the other side of that reality for the protagonist who is the representative of a middle-class man is a revelation which shudders his entire existence. Like the avant-garde playwrights, Sircar sets out to let something new to shock the sensibility of his reader and to make them conscious of the fact that their indifference and do-nothing policy are largely responsible for the present threatening condition of the world they live in.

In the making of *Baki Itihas*, it is the third act that reflects that, in Sircar's mind, the writing of this play is not an easy voyage for him. He states: "*Baki Itihas* needed a more conscious effort—it was one play that gave me a lot of trouble.... I started it and got stuck...for months...I had to invent the stories...and I can never invent stories...for the simple reason that I can't write stories.... But the germ of the third act was already there. In a way, it was a kind of...rewriting of *Ebong Indrajit* that came out in the third act, with a difference. Not the *Myth of Sisyphus*, but the *Baki Itihas*." (Sircar; qtd. in Anjum 60-61)

The play projects various sides of the history of mankind. One side of history comprises violence, bloodshed, mass destruction, the victories of the emperors, kings, heroes, the history full of riots and wars and Hitler and Hiroshima and so on. It is observed that injustice done to man by man has not stopped or reduced. On the contrary, it is continued on a larger scale with magnified violence. Another side has those faceless people on whose shoulders' the heroes put their guns and created the records of their achievements. There is still one more side of history. It comprises a common man with his conventional, humdrum, monotonous routine with day-to-day concerns with a least regard for the other side of history.

Sitanath's statements are the eye-opener for Sharad: "No.... No one can do anything. Oppression, murder, violence, war will continue—all carried out by man, but still there's nothing man can do. The very man who's content with his two meals a day will stab another.... The same scientist who cannot bear to see an animal in pain will invent a weapon of mass destruction.... These are all men. Like you. Like me. They have all tried to find a meaning in life in order to carry on surviving." Sharad is bewildered by this exposure of life. This revelation gives a jerk to his consciousness and makes him sensitive to the issues of life.

Towards the end of the play is the beginning of the audience's consciousness. They are left perplexed. The play's protagonist makes them introspective to this untold other side of history. Sitanath seems to be a minute microcosm of those faceless folks whose names are unknown to society. The realization of the absurdity of his existence incites him to commit suicide. Sir Herbert is quite justified in criticising:

> The problem of our age is not a problem of conscience or commitment—of why people choose to die in wars

> or.... The problem is rather why people who have no personal convictions of any kind allow themselves to suffer for indefinite or undefined causes.... The problem is mass-suffering, mute and absurd.... (Shodhganga 59)

The guilt consciousness of being indifferent to society leaves Sitanath frustrated. The only escape route he finds is in the form of suicide. Actually, Sitanath enjoys a jubilant personal life. But the knowledge of the darker side of history generates a guilt complex in his mind as in the case of Indrajit. In his life "all the past, present and future had fused into one single hopeless subsistence" and that becomes the real cause of his suicide. Sumanta Banerjee rightly points out that Sitanath's "attitude is born of pessimism about humanity, of the belief that tyranny is eternal." (Banerjee; qtd. in Shodhganga 59)

The third version of the story is, actually the sub-conscious or semi-conscious layer of the mind of Sharad. That is why he identifies himself with Sitanath. The strengthening as well as extension of this can be seen in his act of attempting suicide. The photo-album, consisting of the pictures of the scene of violence, slaughter, and bloodbath illustrates to Sharad the history of cruelty from the primitive time to the destruction of millions of people by the use of atom bomb towards the end of the Second World War. Following in the footsteps of Sitanath, Sharad starts pondering over human cruelty with increasing intensity. He experiences vicarious guilt for not having done anything either to improve or to cure the society of its maladies—the suffering, injustice, torture, murder, oppressions, the world wars and the tragedy of Hiroshima.

Actually, his encounter with Sitanath is a part of his own psyche—the true voice of his conscience. It rises to a crescendo and starts suffocating him. Taking the electric lamp cord in his hands he starts a move towards ending his life "but is interrupted by the news of an imminent promotion—and an abrupt return to the reality of domesticity. A garrulous visitor, cups of tea, conversation and chatter. Yet the traces of unease remain. He says, "It was just a useless, false, meaningless nightmare." Yet his last words in the play are a cry of *baki itihas*—the other history that, once having intruded, can never be ignored. (Katyal 62)

Sharing a burden of the knowledge of the other history, his conscience does not allow him to live a life of content. He is left to suffer the agony of living with a consciousness of being the part of the world which is full of "hollow men". His plight is similar to that of the people of Canterbury in *Murder in the Cathedral*, stating: "Yet we have gone on living,/ Living and partly living..." (Part-II, 167-68). "He is at a loss, searching for security in the midst of annihilation, and admits his responsibility for the crimes of humanity. But it does not lead to any action for change from his addiction to routine life. Sircar stops with raising the conscience of the onlookers, leaving the subsequent relevant action in the hands of the individuals themselves." (Shodhganga 60-61)

The structure of the play is experimental. The first two acts deal with the two versions of the story behind Sitanath's suicide. The third act explores the various states of mind of the protagonist in one of which he really tries to commit suicide. The motivation for suicide is not the personal tragedy but a total apathy of the middle-class to the dark side of history.

The class depicted in the play is white-collar middle class one, that is Sircar's "own milieu, with its blinkered existence.... In the earlier play, the process of politicisation was begun, with a questioning and refusal to conform. Here, the demand is more intense—Has the choice to be between action and suicide? Is the domestic middle-class round of daily existence a denial of reality? Whereas action—intervention—was not even a possibility for the protagonists of *Ebong Indrajit*, who were struggling merely to find a reason to carry on, the subject in *Baki Itihas* faces the harsh choice between his personal, every-day routine and the demands of that other, violent, history. Is suicide the only option, then, for the aware middle-class subject?... Badal-da is continuing to mull over this question of the literate middle-class subject and his ability for action or heroism." (Katyal 62-63)

The play ends with producing guilt in each of the audience who are left to ponder over the situation. True that Badal

Sircar's is a Theatre of Conscience in the manner Artaud's is a Theatre of Cruelty.

Works Cited

Banerjee, Sumanta. "The Theatre of Badal Sircar." *Theatre India*, No. 2, November, 1999.

http//shodhganga.inflibnet.ac.in/bitstream/10603/21443/8/08_chapter%202.pdf

Katyal, Anjum. *Badal Sircar: Towards a Theatre of Conscience*. Sage, 2015.

(N.B. All textual quotations are from Katyal, Anjum. *Badal Sircar: Towards a Theatre of Conscience*. Sage, 2015.)

5

Shesh Nei: Looking into "Inner Self"

Introduction

The horrible effects of the atom bomb used in the Second World War have been responsible to change Badal Sircar's perspective on the "ordered existence of middle-class living, with its prescribed narrative of birth, education and career, marriage, procreation, death, in an unbroken loop." (Katyal 220)

This horror of war ultimately makes him lead from the proscenium to the non-proscenium theatre. Sircar firmly believes that the change in the mind-set of people will certainly bring about a revolution in society. So, he is a propagandist and uses theatre as a means of social reform. To develop his theatre as people's theatre, he successfully tries to make it less expensive from the point of view of the audiences, similarly, from that of the performance as well.

Sibaji Bandyopadhyay observes a direct connection between the nuclear criticism and Sircar's adoption of the Third Theatre. He states: "I strongly feel that Badal Sircar's move towards the Third Theatre...would not have taken place, if his reflections on death and disaster had not widened.... The memory of Hiroshima Day and the terrifying apocalypse which would "not only be the final and fullest extension of every cruelty and viciousness but also the annihilation of every possibility of justification or condemnation" haunts many Badal Sircar's plays" (Bandyopadhyay; qtd. in Anjum 221). *Shesh Nei* belongs to the same tradition.

The group of three plays *Baki Itihas* (*That Other History*), *Tringsha Shatabdi* (*The Thirtieth Century*), and *Shesh Nei* (*There's No End*) is called Calcutta Trilogy since each of them is the output of his contemplation of the effects of atom bomb and each of them deals with the cruel absurdities of life, the horrifying effects of nuclear weapon on society, aspirations and frustrations of the ruthless urban generation, man's indifference and callousness to his environment that is going more and more critical, and so on. In Tendulkar's plays, it is observed that the individual is always in conflict with the backdrop of society. Contradictory to it, Sircar represents an individual alienated from society, who remains largely responsible for the present situation, which is increasingly becoming hostile. Veena Noble Dass opines: "A lifelong nagging reminder of guilt can be the only consolation for the Indrajits, Sharadindus and Sumantas who are too sensitive and individualistic to choose any path of action to put an end to Hiroshimas" (Das 68). However, it is observed that in the portrayal of Sumantas' character, Sircar goes a step ahead by showing his shift from victim to judge.

The play *Shesh Nei* can be seen as a prelude to Sircar's shift from proscenium to non-proscenium. It marks a beginning of the questions that he puts forth through his Third Theatre for the audiences to think over, to make them introspective to bring reformation in their thinking modes. Studying the play from this perspective, Rustom Bharucha states: "Though he has diverted considerably from the dramatic structure and the characterization of *Shesh Nei* [in his non-proscenium work], Sircar continues to return the same questions in that play: What is the responsibility of the middle class to the pervasive terror and injustice of this world? What is the role of the individual in collective action? How does one make another person confront his or her guilt without, in some way, concealing one's own? These are difficult questions, which Sircar continues to grapple with in his exploration of the Third Theatre." (Bharucha; qtd. in Anjum 85)

The Structure of the Play

The play opens with Sumati, the close friend of Sumanta, the protagonist opening the door. She is pushed by a crowd of impatient people, women among them, who jostle and enter together. Some are carrying cameras, other garlands, yet others framed felicitations. A few have autograph books. They surround Sumati and starts asking simultaneously about Sumanta.

Sumanta enters there with a gentle smile on his face. The people gathered there are overwhelmed by his success. They feel very proud of him thinking that he is a poet of national fame. They also consider that with his success, "Literature is honoured! Bengal is honoured! India is honoured!" (322)

Sumanta accepts the felicitation and the mob leaves his house. Sumanta has least consideration for success, honour, name, and fame. Actually, at this highest moment of joy, his mind is preoccupied with fear. He confesses to Sumati: "I am afraid. I have a feeling that there is some gap somewhere, some flaw" (334). To make him comfortable, Sumati shifts the table on which the garlands are put in the inner room. When alone, Sumanta goes in a fit of reverie. He is confronted by an unnamed diabolic figure, 'The Man' who commands him to attend his own trial, refusing to explain the charges against him. He brings Sumanta to the dock through hypnosis.

Sumanta finds himself inextricably involved in an unexpected trial. The Man represents six witnesses against him. They include his mother Mrinalini, his girlfriend Manika, his college friend Prasanta, his teacher Prof. Amiya Mukherjee, his former employer N.C. Srivastava, the Branch Manager of S.K. Industries Ltd., and his companion Sumati.

The first five of them accuse him of various 'crimes' of his past life, which are not at all crimes from common man's point of view. His mother condemns him for not taking care of her. Manika accuses him of betraying her in love matter. Prasanta had high expectations from him and thought that with his extraordinary intelligence he could have done a lot in the field of politics. The party needs persons like him. But he left the party and resumed his studies. His teacher, Prof. Amiya complains that he had deprived the sciences by abandoning his quest for research. His former employer had a complaint against him for not utilising his brilliance for the benefit of the firm. Even Sumati his strongest ally is somewhat baffled and cannot speak in favour of him.

Sumanta himself works as the defence council. In his counter arguments, he explains his side in a court, where there is no judge. In his defence, he considers his mother's love as possessive and paralysing: "In the name of protection you built a wall, shut the whole world out and made your son a stunted weakling" (334). This protected life gives him the feeling of suffocation that ultimately leads him to frustration. Prasanta's statement: "the fault lay...in society itself. And that society could be changed,...that would be the only reason for living" (342) saved him from his nervous breakdown. He entered the field of politics with an aspiration to serve and uplift society but the leaders of his party had not contributed to fulfil his dreams of an ideal life. Marriage for him is a great obstacle in his venture. So, he refused to marry Manika, a lady close to his heart.

All the charges against Sumanta indicate the expectation of all the persons related to him. Sumanta never considers himself guilty. Therefore, he tries to prove so. However, his conscience gets disturbed due to this trial. Through this disturbed psyche, five anonymous figures emerge who accuse him for his indifference to society and alienation from it which gets exemplified in his negligence to the beggar, the unemployed worker, the victim of a communal riot and the survivor of an atomic explosion.

It is a trial without a judge to give the final verdict. The play ends with all characters declaring: "We are all the accused!" (396). So, the final verdict is that the trial will go on forever as there is no end to such problems. The best solution lies only in the hands of man.

Critical Interpretation and Appraisal of the Play

Shesh Nei, written in 1970, extends the theme of the earlier plays *Baki Itihas* and *Tringsha Shatabdi*, that is, the theme of guilt-consciousness and responsibility through the character of Sumanta, the play's protagonist.

In *Shesh Nei*, Sircar squeezes the essence of the three plays and concentrates on building one character of Sumanta, the writer. Through his character, one can easily perceive Sircar's concern for the whole humanity—that is, the indifference, lovelessness, callousness of the middle-class individual towards society. Sumanta is the mature version of the protagonists of the earlier plays in that he shares the intellect, sensitivity of Indrajit for the underdogs of the society, guilt-consciousness of Sharad for his inactivity, and tendency of self-introspection and acceptance of guilt of the protagonist of *Tringsha Shatabdi*, where he arranges a trial for the tragedy of Hiroshima, and later accuses himself, too. But in *Shesh Nei*, Sumanta, who is the accused at the beginning of the trial, becomes a judge towards its end to give the final verdict that each one is the accused in this unending trial of life.

The play starts in the manner of the Kafkaesque trial. The protagonist of the play Sumanta is put in the trial stand. He is accused of different kinds of crimes by the people who have been related to him in different roles. According to Sumanta Banerjee, "It is an unequal contest between a rebel and a hostile social environment" (Banerjee 109; qtd. in Anjum 84). His mother, friend, teacher, employer and girl-friend held him guilty for neglecting as well as keeping aside their expectations. Sumanta genuinely feels that his accusers "have merely looked on him as their own reflections, and have tried to deprive him of any identity of his own" (Kulkarni 13). Fulfilling their expectations, for him, is like imprisoning himself in the role in which his lonely spirit would find disgusting and from where there is no return possible. He has successfully escaped by choosing poetry as his medium of self-expression. The life of the poet is in his poetry; the life of an artist is in his art and not in the state of worldly matters. He chooses his own path, which is not at all a crime for him. That is all what he wants to say in his self-defence.

Sumanta is the representative of the educated middle-class young people of the contemporary society. The play is actually just like "looking within our inner-self". Sircar highlights this search of "inner-self" by creating a dream-like setting, indicated on stage by the dim lighting. He successfully explores the unfathomable depth of human psyche. So, it is a voyage in the subconscious. "However, the clear-cut logic so uncharacteristic of the dream with which Sumanta actually maintains his identity, would seem only to prove the opposite. The wholly verbal defence by which Sumanta attempts to mould the reality of his existence, as he criticises his accusers, appears as pointless as the people who seem to be threatening it. For the 'Self' does not emerge through this rationalization and explanation of one's deeds. The words fall empty, as empty as the person delivering them. Both Sumanta and his accusers are victims of the same mania." (Kulkarni 1-14)

Sumanta tries to prove his innocence and overpower the wrong reflections of his accusers. Despite his frantic efforts, he can define himself only in negation. Throughout the trial, his presence does not really emerge, since the 'I' has no basis for existence. The play like the previous one, that is, *Baki Itihas*, makes us realise that we are "the hollow men", "we are the stuffed men". Our 'I' appears to be an empty carcass, static and dead in the presence of others. The play unveils the truth that the 'I' of the past, which Sumanta and his accusers are familiar with has no living reality.

The play presents a trial without a judge. Using this technique, the playwright seems to suggest that we ourselves are the best judges of our deeds in the trial of life. At the subconscious-level, each of us is engaged in the activity of evaluating and judging ourselves. That is why the play ends with all the characters, saying "—we are all the accused!" (396). The total disregard for the court etiquette, which Sircar uses as a theatrical device initiates the ruin of these assumptions and posits the truth of the role. The chaos that is brought into the court reveals a similar chaos in identity: Who is the accused? Who is the witness? The jury? The judge? Everything is mixed up." (Kulkarni 14)

In the same contemplation, Rustom Bharucha, quite justifiably states: "Each individual is the accused and the judge at the same time.... It is a continuous process of self-evaluation and social criticism. Thus, there is no end to the trial—*shesh nei*." (Banerjee 109; qtd. in Anjum 85)

The play best illustrates the philosophy of existentialism. Sumanta, the representative of the middle-class human beings has no 'I' but the roles he assumes as the situation demands. All the accusers in the trial, in this sense are essential for the existence of the self. The root of problem lies in the fact that each one lives on a different level of experience and therefore, makes a choice as per the necessity of situation and cannot fulfil the expectations of all others around him. Sumanta who is an accused at the beginning of the trial, emerges as a judge towards its end only by accident and not by conscious will. The play establishes the fact that "...it is only a conscious choice that paves the way for the making of the self. Not capable of doing this, Sumanta can only justify his nameless existence and give himself up to the trial that will never end." (Kulkarni 14-15)

The concept of static time is also perceptible here. There is a shift from the static to the dynamic. Static time indicates undefined yet predictable texture of time, which resists all change, leaving the consciousness undisturbed and secure. It is basically a result of the man's non-involvement with the world in its real dimensions of time and space. "The play *Shesh Nei* can be described as a reaching towards that zero point, where the 'Self' having stripped of its traditional definition lapses into 'roles' and leaves successively from moment to moment" (Kulkarni 63). All the accusers, who have held Sumanta guilty, are the upholders of static time. So, their relationship with Sumanta no longer forms the part of the present. Sircar, here, seems to criticise the tendency of human beings to live always in past and to remain inactive in the present context. Banerjee Sumanta quite appropriately states: "Though Sircar piles up evidence in support of human responsibility for social evils, he cannot provide stronger justification for the heroes to continue the old way of life." (Shodhganga 68)

Sumanta's journey from accused to judge is very significant. It makes sense in the context of time. His declaration and acceptance at the end of the play "I am the accused..." (396) obliquely symbolises his search for "inner-self" as well as his recognition of self-guilt. To avoid the repetition of the past, this transition is a must. "The past here has a limited relevance in the sense that it is not continued into the present but broken off abruptly.... The consciousness in time makes for an ever-renewed present. In the trial, therefore, there is always a new beginning and the trial can never end" (Kulkarni 64). Looking into the past, we have to take correct decisions at the present, which shows its results in future time and there will be no repetition of the *baki itihas*. This is possible only when we ourselves are the judges of our actions—seems to say the playwright in the garb of the protagonist. To conclude the discussion in the words of Mirza Galib: "It is a great achievement on one's part, if one recognizes oneself."

Works Cited

Bandyopadhyay, Sibaji. Interview with the Author. 17 May 2014.

Banerjee, Sumanta. "The Theatre of Badal Sircar." *Theatre India*. No. 2, Nov. 1999.

Bharucha, Rustom. *Rehearsals of Revolution: The Political Theatre of Bengal*. Seagull, 1983.

Das, Veena Noble. "Experiment and Innovation in Modern Indian Drama in Translation: The Plays of Mohan Rakesh, Badal Sircar, Vijay Tendulkar, and Girish Karnad." *Contemporary Indian Drama*, edited by Sudhakar Pandey and Freya Taraporwala, Prestige, 1990.

Katyal, Anjum. *Badal Sircar: Towards a Theatre of Conscience*. Sage, 2015.

Kulkarni, Jaya. *Modernist Trends in Contemporary Indian Theatre: With Special Reference to Girish Karnad, Mohan Rakesh and Badal Sircar* (in Translation). A Dissertation submitted in partial fulfilment for the degree of M. Litt. Central Institute of English and Foreign Languages.

http://shodhganga.inflibnet.ac.in/bitstream/10603/21443/8/08_chapter%202.pdf

(N.B. All textual quotations are from Sircar, Badal. *There's No End* (317-97), translated by Sarah K. Ensley, occurred in *Modern Indian Plays*. Vol. 1, edited by Chandrasekhar Kambar, National School of Drama, 2000).

6

Pagla Ghoda: Untamed Passion of Love

Introduction

Pagla Ghoda written in 1967 is the only play of Sircar which totally deals with women question. He was about to leave Africa. His mind was pre-occupied with mixed feelings of nervousness for leaving Africa after several years of stay and eagerness for returning to motherland. It is during this emotional turmoil, sensitive phase, that he starts writing *Pagla Ghoda*.

The play is about the life of human beings; the life which consists of such events and incidents as loving, not loving, staying together, making departure, the suffering, joy, sorrow, complex human relationships, and so on. The playwright, here, seems to analyse as well as determine the value and meaning of life. It is a play about a woman in male-dominated Indian society. It depicts the various phases in her life: her childhood, her growing years, her various relationships, her getting apart from that relationships, and her death.

Describing his mental state while writing this play, Sircar states: "Malti, Milli, Lachmi are living people for me now, I can see them in front of me. Have I ever really seen them as separate individuals? But little bits of them were there in all those others—Malti, Milli, Lachmi, and the women without name, who is all three of them in one. Himadri, Shashi, Satkari, Kartik—have I seen them? No. Are they coming through as men, as individual persons? Probably not. There's no need. I am not writing this play with the purpose of creating characters. Then what is my purpose? No purpose. No facts. No theory is being provoked here.... Still I'm writing. And being able to drown in the process of writing, I feel as if I'm writing what is known to me. I know all this." And a month later, after completing the play, he writes: "*Pagla Ghoda* will remain one of my most favourite plays. I was totally immersed in it while writing it." (Sircar 289-90; qtd. in Anjum 74)

The Structure of the Play

In this play, Sircar has used surreal elements on a large scale. The setting of the play is a cremation ground at night. While waiting for the cremation of the corpse of a young woman who has killed herself, the four men entertain themselves by playing cards and drinking liquor. As the night advances, they share their love-stories which indirectly throw light on their guilt-consciousness. Actually, it is the spirit of the young, nameless girl that stimulates and also persuades them to tell their stories. In between, she laments over the total lack of any passion or love in her life. It is this emotional sterility, a barrenness that ultimately led her to commit suicide.

Shashi is a middle-class gentleman. He loves Malti who is supposed to be marrying his childhood friend Pradip. She genuinely requests him to marry her further telling him the fact sincerely that she cannot marry a person whom she does not love. Shashi can neither go against the current nor can break his friendship. Even her showing him of the evidence of physical abuse, Pradip has given her for narrating the fact that she is in love with Shashi and therefore, hates him (Pradip). To the arguments raised by Malti, Shashi remains helpless: "You reject me just for this—for Pradip?...just because you will lose face with him?" His friendship, the older relationship between the two men—the brotherhood is more important for him than his love. He tries to console her, saying: "Not with Pradip Malti. Myself. I will lose respect for myself. If I lose to myself like this and marry you, I will never be able to be happy myself and neither will I be able make you happy."

He not only refuses to marry Malti but compels her to marry Pradip saying, the thought that he came between her and his best friend will be preoccupied in his mind and will perturb him forever. Unable to change his point of view and to remove his ego, his self-esteem she gives up the relationship and returns to her hellish abode just to end herself. Contemplating on the situation, Shashi comes to the conclusion that not Malti's cruel husband but he himself is responsible for her death. He lives with guilt and remorse. Sircar here denounces our high sounding moral stance that is totally hollow and hypocritical.

Himadri and Milli fell in love with each other. He is the youngest of the four men and used to work as a tutor to the Milli's brother. Class-consciousness remains the greatest barrier in their love matter, the culmination of which is marriage. Milli hails from a wealthy, Westernised family. 'Tennis, swimming, driving, party-picnics' is her life. He cannot accept her with her positive and negative traits. Instead, he remains highly critical of her habit of drinking. These cultural differences resulted from their distinct classes keep him away from committing fully to her. Her pleading and assuring that she will try her best to change herself as per his expectation, come to nothing. He leaves her once and forever even resigning the duty as a tutor. Broken-hearted, she meets a tragic accident for driving a car too fast under the influence of liquor. The love story again ends with the feeling of guilt and remorse.

Satu is a road-Romeo one amongst them—entertaining the friends with liquor, always ready with gross and daring comments. He is a contractor by profession. Possessing a natural lust to enjoy life, he neglects socio-cultural norms and dictates and therefore, has remained a bachelor. He boasts, "Why bother getting married when I can get the benefits without it?" He looks quite rough and tough in his appearance, way of talking and behaving which he makes no attempt to disguise. He also unveils his love-story to his friends.

Lachmi is the woman he rescued from enslavement. Now, she is in love with him and wants nothing better than serve and look after him. But he finds her a job and sends her to perform her duty. However, she comes to him for protection one night, clearly terrified, and pleads him to take her in. But he refuses telling her that he cannot possibly have her live with him being scared of 'what people will say' and sends her back.

"Is it fear of commitment that holds him back or fear of scandal? The next time he sees her, she is a corpse. She has died destitute, sick, alone. He is left with questions—was it wrong to rescue her in the first place and raise her expectations? Was it wrong to entrust her to others? Again, guilt and responsibility, and the failure to love." (Katyal 206)

The last one among the four is Kartik. He is a chemist, a compounder by profession. Early in the play, he shares an anecdote about a man who spent his whole life loving someone from her childhood to grown-up age. It was a one-sided love that remained undeclared. Later it is observed that the devoted lover is no one but Kartik himself, and the unnamed girl who is being cremated is his so-called beloved. Once she declares to Kartik her longing for death as she had nothing to live for. Being ignorant of Kartik's love, she thinks that she neither loved nor is loved by anybody. So, there is no reason to continue such a type of barren life. Shaken, he extracts a promise from her that she will wait for a week. However, within the week, he comes across the news of her suicide by strangling herself.

Kartik has lost his chance at love as well as that of making her feel to be loved. She dies without a satisfaction that someone was genuinely in love with her. This fact might have been proved an oasis for her to continue life. Kartik's inability to express his passion of love may be either due to his inner weakness or the social restraints he himself had imposed on himself becomes the cause of their tragedy.

Critical Interpretation and Appraisal of the Play

The plot of the play revolves round four men, who have gathered at the funeral of an unknown young woman who has killed herself for the cause of love. The play focuses on man-woman relationships and highlights the subjugation of women in a patriarchal system. It skilfully explores the relationships of men and women from four different socio-economic segments of society. Here, the playwright, quite obliquely suggests that regardless of education and background, men are the same, that is, quite rough and indifferent in their handling of passion, love, and women.

Like *Evam Indrajit*, *Baki Itihas, Shesh Nei*, this play also criticises middle-class man's inability to break society's norms and dare to take an anti-establishment stance, an emotional risk. The locale depicted is the middle-class one and all the four women are emotionally honest and true to themselves, possessing a natural lust for life and also the courage to devote their life for the cause of love. Although the characters belong to the different strata of society, none of these characters emerge as multi-dimensional, neither the women nor the men. On the other hand, all of them appear rather flat, one-dimensional. Sircar, like in many other plays, here remained fiercely critical for the Bengali middle-class man's skin-defence tendency. Anjum Katyal's statement in this regard goes thus: "The play sets out to make a point—that Bengali middle-class men are social and emotional cowards, forever ruled by the fear of 'what others will think', and given no calculation rather than passion; and that as a result, they do not have the capacity to truly love, since love demands passion, that one lose oneself in something much bigger than oneself." (Katyal 74)

The play is melodramatic in nature. Its theme is derived from a popular Bengali rhyme. *Pagla Ghoda*, that is, a wild or mad horse signifies a force out of control, unpredictable and terrible in its untamed beauty. This force, which can shake one's existence, is repeatedly used by the spirit of the dead woman which shows her craze for the passion of love. All the women characters in the play symbolised by the image of *Pagla Ghoda* stand exact opposite to the careful, cautious men characters who do not dare to go against the current and take a risk in fear of social disapproval.

Pagla Ghoda throws light on Sircar's progressive, leftist ideology. It fiercely criticises the so-called cultured society where women are always taken for granted. All the four male characters in the play are the upholders of the conventional, exploitative social order following its norms and traditions, allowing themselves to be dictated by it. They are portrayed as severely calculating in their relationship at the cost of their hearts and desires. That is why they are ready to sacrifice the woman they love rather than to take a risk that may cause scandal and outrage or result in creating turmoil in their life and ultimately result in losing their reputation.

It is observed that all the women in this play, in the matter of love remain bold, courageous, sincere, and devoted while all the four men appear hypocrite, coward and insincere. That is why all of them have betrayed the women in their lives. These women are the perfect images of true love offering themselves unconditionally, daring to love without any reservation and ready to face the calamities and the ultimate consequences in the way as well. Each of them sacrifices her life for the noble cause of love. Contrary to it, the men are portrayed as idiosyncratic individuals with their distinct characters sharing stories and experiences, teasing each other, playing cards and drinking together, that is also at the cremation of the corpse of a young woman who faces a tragic death.

Malti, Milli, and Lachmi, although belong to different locale, could be interchangeable. They are the witnesses of womankind's endless suffering in the male-dominated society. All of them die for the cause of love. Milli is somewhat distinct from the other three in the sense that she shows a hint of boldness in the way of living life and in facing death also. The overwhelming impression created in the play is: "love, and a relationship with a man, is the only thing that gives (sic. man, are the only things that give) value to a woman's life. She is incomplete, empty, of no value, unless a man ascribes her value by claiming her.... In this play women are modern enough to aspire to romantic love, and to express their desire to their men, but they remained defined by what the men are not—they are indicative of a lack in the male." (Katyal 207-08)

While speaking about the female characters in the play Sibaji Bandyopadhyay states: "Sircar's treatment of women is a repetition of a very old paradigm which is part and parcel of Bengal's modernity. The entire scheme of modernity of Bengal was articulated through the figure of the woman. So, the woman is in most cases a kind of storehouse of various desires—an empty signifier." (Bandyopadhyay; qtd. in Anjum 208)

The character of the fourth woman—who remains unnamed—is distinct a little bit from the other in the sense that she remains present throughout the play. It is she who constantly persuades the four men to tell the stories of their life and compels them revisiting their memories, making them introspective and leaving them with the sense of guilt. Her constant invoking of the *pagla ghoda* metaphor, that is, the wild horse of untamed passion, shows her unfulfilled desire of love. It is only after death, she comes to know that someone was in genuine love with her. She meets the *pagla ghoda* in the journey from where no return is possible.

Throughout the play, there is a powerful plea for women, that is, to treat them as human beings. Although their depiction is one-dimensional as the pathetic, suffering figure, they leave the spectators disturbed. Sircar has provided a commentary on many burning issues in the life of women. The institution of marriage is attacked which, in many cases gives men license to mistreat women. It is also observed that financial dependency is responsible for the exploitation of women to a large extent. To conclude the discussion in the words of G.J.V. Prasad: "In *Pagla Ghoda*, you don't have a play about what men do to men, which is vintage (sic. in/of) Sircar, but what men do to women. Thus, it has a unique place in Sircar's oeuvre." (Prasad; qtd. in Anjum 208)

Works Cited

Bandyopadhyay, Sibaji. Interview with the Author. 17 May 2014.

Katyal, Anjum. *Badal Sircar: Towards a Theatre of Conscience*. Sage, 2015.

Prasad, G.J.V. Interview with the author. 30 May 2014.

Sircar, Badal. *Prabasher Hijibiji.* (Trans.), quoted in Anjum Katyal.

(N.B. All textual quotations are from Katyal, Anjum. *Badal Sircar: Towards a Theatre of Conscience*. Sage, 2015).

7

Spartacus: A Phoenix for the Slaves

> I could feel that with *Spartacus* we made a giant leap towards a closer relationship with the audience.
>
> (Badal Utsav 9; qtd. in Anjum 124)

The landmarking play *Spartacus* shows Sircar's successful voyage from proscenium to Anganmanch. Actually, it is not the first play to be produced at Anganmanch. Before it, Sircar has used *Anganmanch* for *Sangina Mahato* and *Evam Indrajit*. But this form of theatre reaches to its climax since the performance of *Spartacus*.

The play deals with the story of the Roman slave revolt in 71 B.C. It is based on the novel with the same title by Howard Fast one of Sircar's favourite books. He has a desire to dramatise it and could do it only with his shift from the conventional to the Third Theatre. The subject of the play, in the words of the playwright, goes thus:

Spartacus is the story of the great slave revolt that began in BC 71 and shook the mighty Roman Empire for four long years. Although it began from a spontaneous upsurge in the gladiatorial school of Capua, it did not remain so for long. Under the able leadership of Spartacus, the gladiator, the handful of rebels soon transformed into an organised slave army of thousands which fought for something unheard of by any other army the world had seen so far. In the words of Howard Fast...it was an army which fought for freedom in the most simple and unvarnished terms. In the past, there have been armies without end, armies which have fought for nations or cities or wealth or spoils or power or control of this or that area; but here was an army which fought for human freedom and dignity, an army which called no land or city of its own, because the people within it came from all lands and cities and tribes, an army where every soldier shared a common heritage of servitude and a common hatred of men who made other men slaves. This was an army which was committed to victory, for there were no bridges over which it could retreat, no land which would give it shelter or rest. It was an army which suddenly had the knowledge that the victory to which it was committed must change the world and, therefore, the army must change the world or have no victory. The army was crushed ultimately, because the majority of the slaves would not or could not join it; apart from thousands killed in the fields of battle, over 6,000 captured slaves were crucified along Via Appia as punishment. (Sircar 115)

What is important for Sircar is not history but the message of this history. It makes the event relevant to him. He continues: "But the war of the oppressed against those who oppressed them went on. It was a flame which burned high or low but never went out—and the name of Spartacus did not perish.... And this descent of Spartacus makes the story relevant in any part of the world at any time." (Sircar 35)

Thus, the play, although it is based on the ancient historical event, crosses the boundaries of historicity and temporality. The picture, depicted in the play, is common to all periods and societies. In this connection, Rustom Bharucha states: "The war of the oppressed continues in our century in Cambodia, Afghanistan, and elsewhere in the world, while repressive regimes have survived the rising of the proletariat." (Bharucha 150-51; qtd. in Anjum 121)

Making of the Play

The writing of this play is different from that of the other plays. Sircar himself narrated that the first draft of this play was quite long. It required four hours for performance although he reluctantly left out some sequences and characters which were important from his point of view. He did not try at all to edit the script. During the workshop, rehearsals were arranged. He had discussions with the group, and following trial and error method, changes and modifications were made as per the comments and suggestions of the members. He himself had decided that, except in rare cases of unresolved controversy, the final choreography would depend on the decision of the group rather than that of his own opinions as the director. Any type of compromise was not made while deleting the sections and lines of the content. While cut-shorting the size of the play, the verbosity of the script was shortened. Pages of the script began to be replaced by "expression through sound, movement and energy" (Sircar 104). Gradually, the script got shortened. This new method of editing the script made the play experimental and avant-garde in nature.

As stated at the outset, the play marks a definite break with the previous proscenium plays. Sircar has written it particularly for Anganmanch, that is, keeping the features of theatre-in-the-round in mind. The play does not have individual characters; rather it has groups—that of the slaves, the Roman soldiers, and a few Roman characters who are more archetypes and not characters. The play is not divided into acts and scenes. Instead, it comprises very short scenes, even sometimes ending just in a minute or two. Any type of expenditure was not made on the sets or props or dressing or lighting. Effective use of music was made as a refrain but that is also without any instrumental accompaniment. This refrain without words, hardly six or seven notes, sung by the slaves communicates their suffering and determination more efficiently than words.

The whole play revolves round five actions, that is, capturing of the people, selling of these captives in the market, slaves toiling, gladiator-slaves fighting in the arena, and crucifixion of the slaves for the act of rebellion. Instead of dialogues, cries, shouts and noises were used in these scenes. It is the first play, where Sircar has used human body to develop the action of the play. However, for this experiment, a lot of training, practice, and patience were devoted by the team. The members responded positively to the call of the group-leader. The hard work on the part of both the director and the members ultimately leads to the creation of the epoch-making play, a milestone in Sircar's canon.

The play lessens the distance between the actors and spectators. As the play was performed not in an auditorium but in an open space, the gulf between the performers and the audience was bridged. Due to this arrangement of seats, they did not remain just the detached, passive observers but became the part of the performance. What the audience have here, is not just a spectacle but a theatrical experience, which leaves them totally disturbed and compels them to think, feel and meditate. At the end of the play, Sircar makes the actors crawling through the lanes, touching the knees of the spectators, whispering "abar phire ashbo, that is, We will return". After observing the performance of the play, Samik Bandyopadhyay states: "...the actors becoming a physical transmission of the concept, was very powerful. I remember it as one of the greatest moments of theatre. We were drawn into the theatre space" (Bandyopadhyay; qtd. in Anjum 123). In this sense, this play can be considered a prelude, a firm step forward to the Third Theatre.

Sircar and his team tried their best to impart sincerity and honesty to the events of the play. While elucidating the experiences of the rehearsal, Sircar says: "We took as much care as possible to avoid faking. In our workouts, a slave who would mime carrying a load practised carrying another person on his back (mostly me), and he would exert himself just as much during a performance when he would actually be carrying nothing at all. The slaves combined themselves in such a way that each step taken by the group was really painful for the actors and that was how we tried to convey the impression of chained slaves being led over the hot desert sands." (Sircar 105)

For the preparation of the play, "Satabdi" group devoted one year. The first performance of the play took place at Anganmanch on 28th January 1973. It was hailed by the audience with overwhelming response. People's reaction to the play was expressed in the words that they felt the direct impact of the play in a way that they had never experienced in theatre before. The audience included the people of different strata of society such as middle-class, urban educated theatre-going crowd, students, as well as poor, uneducated, illiterate people who watched the whole performance with pin-drop silence and full concentration.

The ending of the play is in perfect harmony with the events depicted in it creating the everlasting impression on the spectators' minds. It ends with all the slaves rising together. Their gesture of rising signifies their hero, Spartacus who has given them the voice of revolt and has devoted his life to the cause of freedom. Spartacus becomes the symbol of all those people who have been striving, struggling, rebelling, and asserting for liberty up to their last drop of blood throughout history, right till the present. The characters take a departure with a message that "Spartacus will come back, reborn among millions of people" Remembering the influence of the ending of the play, the theatre director Probir Guha says: "My hair stood on end. Even today I can remember every scene." (Qtd. in Anjum 120)

Critical Interpretation and Appraisal of the Play

The play is a tragedy but it differs from the Aristotelian concept of the same. When it opens, Spartacus is already dead. It deals with the question "what killed him". The playwright's objective here is to generate understanding through reasoning. Like other plays of Sircar, it leaves the audience introspective and compels them to ponder over the situation. Generally, the conventional tragic hero has an inborn defect in his personality leading him towards his catastrophe. Here, Spartacus faces a death, not due to any fatal flaw in his personality, but rather due to the social situation, the situation which is the result of human thrust for power and man's tendency of getting a sadistic pleasure in inflicting miseries on others! Spartacus becomes a martyr for the cause of liberty. He tries his best to overthrow the Roman Empire which is the symbol of tyranny, oppression and exploitation but remains unsuccessful in it due to the historical and social situation in which he is placed. Spartacus died but is not defeated. He passes away by creating a spirit of revolution in the minds of his predecessors to go against the establishment to change the order. His fight is not a single-handed fight for personal cause. It is a fight for a common good, where the goal can be achieved through common struggle. The play does not at all try to destroy the notion of disaster or calamity; instead it imparts courage to face it boldly. The playwright, it seems, aims at reasserting the principle of regeneration. That is why the whispering of the slaves that "I will return again in millions and millions" is transformed into a crescendo of assertion.

The play, though has a fixed theme, is absurd in nature. There is no sequence in the narrative; the two events belong to the same time are put backward and forward and sometime two different spaces and time are put together in the same scene. The play is named after the name of the character. But he is not delineated as an individual hero. He is the representative of the voice of rebellion against injustice in the society. It is observed that on many occasions, the lines of his most crucial speech are divided between all the slaves. That, too, is a part of its symbolic structure.

In this play, Sircar makes a change in his art of characterization. His characters are not the victims of their psychological state; rather they are the victims of the social situation. It is observed that, in his earlier phase, Sircar was more concerned with the abstract universality of his characters (Amal, Vimal, Kamal, Indrajit in *Evam Indrajit*). In this play, all the characters including Spartacus appear as types and prototypes. They can be replaced or identified with the "group". In Sircar's own words, "For a long time, I have been trying to break through this system of 'story' and 'characters' and in my plays 'theme' and 'types', respectively, began to replace them gradually. Working on the third theatre I began discovering new possibilities of using 'groups' more than either 'characters' or 'types'." (Qtd. in Anjum 99)

From this perspective Spartacus is not the protagonist or the hero of the play. On the other hand, the slaves, striving to change the situation are the heroes. The identification of Spartacus with the group of slaves is achieved marvellously establishing the success of the revolt indicating that the potential to become a future Spartacus is inbuilt within every member of the slave community. It shows Sircar's shift from particular to general. Here, "the group is given greater prominence moving the focus from the total subjectivity of the earlier period to the notion of the collective subject in his later phase." (Chukerbutty 100-01)

The play slightly hints at the women's question. The only female character in the play the wife of Spartacus is showed narrating the plight of the slaves' wives by telling how a slave woman becomes the victim of the gang rape and sacrifices her life.

With *Spartacus*, Sircar tries to develop in the audience a sense of pattern in social relations. It is done with assigning meaning to history. Spartacus, a slave for three generations, is converted into a gladiator by the Masters. The order went topsy-turvy when the gladiators decide to desist from killing one another: the result of a sense of community. Spartacus' significance lies not in his martyrdom but in the capacity of creating the spirit of revolution. Here, the social action emerges from a group of 'men', and not 'man' by himself acting alone.

It seems that Sircar here is trying to bring to notice the meaning of freedom in the true sense of that word. Divide and rule is the policy always used by the oppressors to hold their grip fast on the oppressed. In the action of the play, it is indicated that one slave has been given the right to possess a weapon to kill his opposing gladiator, making him believe that he was a free man. It is Spartacus who creates a consciousness in them: "United we stand and divided we fall." "...their collective decision to abstain from killing one another established for the first time their true freedom necessitated out of their common sense of oppression. This sense of freedom achieved through their negation (to kill) was not dictated by any subjective rhetoric of the heart. It was the result of historical necessity and was not just a freely chosen mode of behaviour." (Chukerbutty 101-02)

The play is considerably branched off to history and contemporary period. The class of the slaves and that of the masters indicate the division of society on the basis of hierarchy which is the permanent characteristic feature of all societies in all periods. It also throws light on man's innate thrust for power. These two classes do not represent individual 'heroes' and 'villains'. On the other hand, they highlight the universal aspect of power and oppression. The play gives a message that ultimate upshot of oppression is resistance and revolt. The actors are clothed in contemporary costume. The dressing establishes the direct relevance of historical event to the contemporary situation. Anjum Katyal rightly points out: "By making the slaves symbolic of the underclass that has risen in rebellion throughout the centuries, Sircar emphasises the historic continuity of inequality and exploitation." (Katyal 122)

The play is full of violence and sensation. Rustom Bharucha states: "It is difficult to imagine a production so violent and yet so rigorous.... In the very first moment of the play, one is simply thrust into a world of terror and brutality.... The relentless movement of the actors as they raise their hands and thrash them down in unison conveys the sheer agony of the slaves' labour. Apart from watching them toil, we see the slaves being captured by a group of anonymous Roman soldiers who look like the military police in Calcutta—impassive, steely eyed, and ruthless.... The most savagely choreographed scenes depict the fight of the slaves in the arena.... After the fight, a slave is crucified for an act of defiance. The raising of his body in the air, the outstretched hands of the slaves in a semicircle, their faces turned upward—all are images that remain with the audience long after the production of *Spartacus* ends." (Bharucha 149-50; qtd. in Anjum 120-21)

The play, although it is marked by bloodshed, massacre, violence, ends on an optimistic note. The lines uttered by the slaves reveal Sircar's dream of the Utopian society in the years to come:

At the beginning of creation, all men were equal. Today because of Rome

> Man has two classes—Master and Slave...
> But no longer, that's all over
> We will destroy your Rome...
> Then we'll build a beautiful town...
> Without walls or barriers...
> Only peace and happiness.

Works Cited

Badal Utsav pamphlet brought out by Natya Shodh Sansthan on the occasion of Badal Utsav, 15-19 July 2009.

Bandyopadhyay, Samik. Interview with the Author. 9 February 2009.

Bharucha, Rustom. *Rehearsals of Revolution: The Political Theatre of Bengal*. Seagull, 1983.

Katyal, Anjum. *Badal Sircar: Towards a Theatre of Conscience*. Sage, 2015.

Sircar, Badal. *On Theatre*. Seagull, 2009.

Chukerbutty, Pronoti. *Phases in the Development of Realism in the 20th Century Drama: A Comparative Study of the Theatre in Bengal and Britain*. A Dissertation submitted in partial fulfilment of the requirement for the degree of Master of Letters in English Literature. C.I.E.F.L., Hyderabad. Sept. 1982.

(N.B. All the quotations of the text are taken from Katyal, Anjum. *Badal Sircar: Towards a Theatre of Conscience*. Sage, 2015.)

The Later Phase: Non-proscenium Plays

8

From the Proscenium Theatre to the Third Theatre

Badal Sircar stands at the forefront of a new theatre movement in India (Dutta 1). He successfully prefers to develop his own theatre in keeping with the demands of his times. His genuine interest in drama since his youth, ultimately leads to his active participation in the theatre regarding the performance of the plays. Initially, he started a rehearsal club with his friends for mere recreation. This club, later on, gradually began to perform full-scale productions. But he felt terribly disappointed with the available set of plays. For him, these plays seemed to be turgid since they were full of melodrama and sentimentality. The upshot of it was that he began to write plays for his rehearsal club. Ella Dutta points out, "Although famous all over India as a playwright, Sircar dismisses his contribution to theatre writing—'I prefer doing theatre to writing theatre. Writing is quite laborious for me'—and he claims that he started writing plays as a matter of expediency." (Dutta 2)

Sircar started his professional career as a civil engineer at Maithon in the Damodar Valley Corporation complex in 1953. He moved to England in 1957 where he worked and studied for two years. In 1963, he visited France to study town planning. After staying in Calcutta for a brief period, he had been to Nigeria in 1964. It was while working there that he wrote quite a few major proscenium plays of his early career which include: *Baki Itihas* (That Other History, 1965), *Tringsha Shatabdi* (The Thirtieth Century, 1966), and *Pagla Ghoda* (The Crazy Horse, 1967).

There are three strands in Sircar's life which intertwine to lend a striking texture to his work and introduce a new value to Indian theatre: (i) his professional career as town planner along with his training as a civil engineer; (ii) his life as a dramatist; and (iii) his role as a theatre director and actor.

Born in Calcutta in 1925, Sircar belongs to the middle-class of the society. Being born and brought up in Calcutta, he has an intimate feel of the urban conscience of this city and has profound understanding of the middle-class life. He describes Calcutta as "a monster of a city, but a monster that is alive, throbbing with vitality and viciousness, may be vision too" (Dutta 2). Through almost all his major plays, he is found probing into the Calcutta middle-class mind. In his plays, he gives expression to the major concerns, aspirations and frustrations of this "little big man" in urban environment. It is for this reason that four of his early major plays: *Evam Indrajit, That Other History, Tringsha Shatabdi,* and *There's No End* are called Calcutta quartet.

Sircar is interested in the responsibility of mankind for the events of present time. He is of the opinion that it is not human being but society that needs to be reformed first. It is out of this interest that he has involved himself in the trade union movement that made him aware of the working class condition. But soon he gets disappointed due to some rash decisions, taken without proper homework. Disillusioned, he gradually returns to theatre—his childhood passion.

Sircar wants to reform society by changing the mind-set of people. The five proscenium plays that he writes from 1963 to 1970, *Evam Indrajit, Baki Itihas, Tringsha Shatabdi, Sarkas,* and *Sesh Nei* reflect his refusal to accept society as it is and his frantic search for the right path to follow. "The central theme of many of his early plays is a sense of utter meaninglessness in our existence which leads to a state of metaphysical anguish. This anguish is in fact closely embedded in the Bengali middle-class psyche, the tearing of which was Sircar's constant concern in his early theatre career." (Dass 66-67)

With *Evam Indrajit* Sircar becomes famous in Indian theatre circles. The play reveals a profound melancholic note in Sircar's writing. It is with the publication and performance of this play, that theatre practitioners all over India become aware of a major talent. The play proves for them the shock of recognition. It is about the Indian reality as they know it. According to Satyadev Dubey, "...it was a theatrically effective and crystallized projection of all the prevalent attitudes, vague feelings and undefined frustrations growing at the hearts of the educated urban middle class" (Dubey ii). The angry and frustrated protagonist of the play (Indrajit) is the true representative of the misfit of the prevailing social order. This peculiar temperament of the protagonist makes the spectators introspective. In his protest against the society, they find the realities of their lives.

Majority of Sircar's protagonists encounter the issue faced by Indrajit, i.e.: Would he fight and motivate others against such injustice? The protagonists fail to resolve this dilemma till the end since they remain undecided about the course of action to take.

It is observed that none of Sircar's serious plays fit into the category of the well-made plays. There is no linear story that gradually reaches to its climax. The play does not have the beginning, the middle, and the end. It ends where it begins. "Besides, the characteristic features of Sircar's later plays—the episodic plot, minimum use of props, actors directly addressing the audience, the role of Stage Managers in carrying the plot forward, an actor appearing in two or more roles—are all present here." (Sarkar xvi)

After writing and directing such plays for the conventional stage for about twenty years during the fifties and the sixties, Sircar pioneered the Third Theatre in the early seventies. With the establishment of this theatre, he wants to create an awareness of exploitation in rural India in the minds of urban audience and also he wants to make the rural audience conscious about their vigour, vitality, and power. The reason for coming out of the proscenium stage is a question in his mind—How can actors communicate directly with the audience? And the answer is: through the Third Theatre. Naturalistic theatre and cinema, for him, separate the audience and the actors. He states: "To the performers, the spectators constitute an anonymous mass, a faceless crowd and, to the spectator, the performers constitute a band of select skilled people—an instrument of entertainment. The human element is absent." (Sircar, *Third* 22)

To make the audience think rationally and to help them to remain critically aware, Sircar thinks that the audience should be in direct touch with the actors and, hence, should be the active participants in the performance. He wants to share with his audience the experience of the joint human action.

The formation of the Third Theatre has a long history and it is quite interesting to trace out the phases in the growth and development of this new form of theatre.

In 1969, Sircar has reorganised his theatre group Satabdi. The first production of this group was *Pralap*. It was subsequently followed by *Sararattir, Shesh Nei,* and *Ballavpurer Rupkatha.* All these plays were written in the conventional style. When he wrote *Sangina Mahato* in 1971, a play based on a Bengali short story, his way of thinking was changed entirely. He gave up the conventional mechanical division of the play into acts and scenes, the sequence of time and the barriers and limitations of space. He used stage to exhibit distinct locales and distinct times simultaneously. At the same, he emphasized group acting, pantomime, rhythmic movements, songs, and dances and, in this way, reduced the importance of language to a large extent. The sets were so simple that they could be easily carried about anywhere or be erected without problems.

At the time of the staging of *Sangina Mahato*, Sircar got conscious of the fact that the time and situation required him to leave proscenium theatre and that this was a play specifically suited for that decision.

The first experimental presentation of the play outside of the proscenium theatre took place on 24th October 1971, at the All Bengal Teacher's Association hall in Calcutta. Here Sircar made the arrangement of creating the acting area in the midst of the spectators and filled the gulf between the performers and the spectators. This new form of performance was welcomed by the spectators with great enthusiasm which gave Sircar a confidence that he was on right path towards the creation of the Third

Theatre. However, the group faced a great deal of difficulties. The ABTA hall was not available for the next four months and further more the availability would be uncertain and irregular.

After the successful performance of the play *Abu Hossain,* Sircar turned to write a new play *Spartacus* which was conceived for the first time entirely for the Third Theatre. The whole process of writing and the performance of the play took the period of one year. In February 1972, Sircar and his group started working on *Spartacus*. Being the writer, he did not take the opportunity of editing the script; instead, he put it to the group "who confronted the script, tried it, tested it, accepted, enriched and rejected it and gradually began to build a structure that was much more than the written script. Through the process, the group was transformed into a workshop in the true sense of the term.... The whole process was necessarily slow; the group was not just *rehearsing* a play set down in definite terms by the playwright but *confronting* a script to create live theatre out of it" (Sircar, *On* 24-25). Observing the positive efforts of the members, Sircar had a feeling that the next play might not be written by him but be created by his Satabdi group.

Sircar considers human body as the most important element in the theatre. So, he steadily reduces the use of sets, props, and costumes and also discards the use of mechanical devices like tape-recorders and projectors. To give the group members a proper training in the workshop where physical acting had the most significant role, Sircar himself went to USA to participate in the various theatre workshops. These workshops and visits to the scholarly personalities in the field such as Scheners, Julian Beck and Judith Malina of the Living Theatre (which very rarely uses theatre halls; even when it does. Similarly, it believes in living in community, accepting theatre as a way of life rather than a profession or a past-time) and Andre Gregory of the Manhattan Project proved helpful to Sircar in formulating and defining his ideas and concepts of the new form of theatre.

After his return from USA, Sircar started his experiments in the Third Theatre in June 1972. He named the theatre Anganmanch, which roughly means 'space theatre'.

What follows here is the brief summary of what Sircar illustrated while describing his ideas about the Anganmanch in the manifesto he himself has drafted:

Anganmanch, run by Shatabdi, is an intimate theatre in flexible form where performers and spectators are intermingled to minimize the distance.

Anganmanch has no commercial purpose. So, instead of buying-selling of ticket it accepted the system of membership.

It is expected that a member joins the organization as a positive participant in this community effort of building a new theatre.

In a year, a minimum of three plays will be presented in the new form, and regular shows will be run each week. The number of shows per week will depend on the response of members.

Every attempt will be made to arrange more than the minimum of three productions, either by Satabdi or by other theatre groups interested in experimenting in this new form.

The membership subscription is ₹ 6 annually. The admission fee is ₹ 4 for the first 300 members and ₹ 6 for the next 200 members.

Each member is entitled to free entry to three shows of Anganmanch within the membership period. Thereafter a nominal entry fee of ₹ 1 for each show is charged.

Guests accompanied by members can see any show on payment of ₹ 3 each. The number of guests may have to be regulated in the case of a new production till all members get a chance to see it.

A non-member is to pay ₹ 5 for entry to show provided seats are available after serving members and their guests.

Life-membership fee is ₹ 200. A life-member can see any show with one companion totally free of cost. (Sircar, *On* 30-31)

The formal opening of Anganmanch took place on 5th November 1972 and from 12th November regular weekly shows started every Sunday. The first play performed here was *Sangina Mahato*.

In order to increase the closeness of the performers and the spectators, the flat backless seats-system was adopted rejecting the chairs. They are of three different heights: low (of 10 in. high), ordinary (of 1 ft. 6 in. high) and high (of 2 ft. 4 in. high). These three levels were adequate to ensure a good view for all. All these seats were arranged on all sides. This system brought the spectators within the theatre.

In the performance of the play, ordinary lights of 100 W, 60 W and 40 W from many sources were used instead of the spot lights from the few sources. Sircar narrated: "We fixed a grid of wire-ropes near the ceiling and hung 16 specially constructed lampshades with clamps. The shades could be shifted along the wire grid to different positions and the clamps allowed them to be turned at any desired angle" (Sircar, *On* 33). The total cost was less than ₹ 300. The professional operator in the proscenium theatre was substituted by the members of the group.

To solve the room's echo problem, Sircar hung pleated canvas curtain on the blank portion of the hall instead of the acoustic treatment. It served dual purpose: it provided a decorative effect and prevented the glare by covering the white-washed walls.

At the very outset, Anganmanch received a considerably favourable response of the 325 ordinary and 14 life-members. It first started with the performance of *Sangina Mahato* and *Evam Indrajit* followed by *Spartacus* on 28th January 1973. This play was mainly based on physical acting for which the group members went through a rigorous training. Here Sircar remained successful in achieving the nearness with the spectators which was totally impossible in a conventional proscenium stage production.

On 17th March 1973, *Spartacus*'s abridged version of just eight minutes which was still a self-contained play in itself was performed by Satabdi in daylight at the open air theatre without a stage, curtains, dressing room, or sets at Surendranath Park. It was attended by more than 500 people with absolute silence and concentration. The performance of the play in the company of flora and fauna such as the grass covered earth, the sun in the sky, the people sitting on the ground—imparted the play a new meaning. "The bits of dry grass and patches of dirt on the bare bodies of the slaves covered with sweat, accentuated by spots of blood from the scratches caused by pebbles on the ground, made it a play of blood and sweat as it was supposed to be" (Sircar, *On* 38). These various performances of *Spartacus* liberated the Third Theatre from the bondage of stage, auditorium, lighting, sets, props, and the cost involved. This remained to be a very important event in the formation of the Third Theatre.

After the completion of the first tenancy, the Academy authorities wanted to increase the rent by 60 per cent. Anganmanch could not afford that. Similarly, the Satabdti team was performing plays free of cost at Surendranath Park and in villages. The team got attracted towards this free theatre not just because the countrymen are poor but also due to the fact that in theatre, both the performers and spectators should have the equal status. They should be totally free in their relationship and that any external factor should not affect it. Admission with cost creates *buyer-seller* relationship which further gets more accentuated by the distinct charges of the tickets as per the seating arrangement. Naturally, the free theatre, "where the people come and stay at will and donate voluntarily (or not at all) after the performance, became our (sic., the team's) choice" (Sircar, *On* 49). Eventually, Sircar's team took departure from the room at the Academy in September 1974, and proceeded further to start the phase of free open-air theatre.

Sircar opines if the theatre has to have a role in creating awareness among people regarding the prevalent socio-economic oppression, the play has to be performed among workers and peasants who usually cannot afford the luxury of paying to attend a show. So, after leaving the room at the Academy, Sircar remains stuck to the open-air format. The play could be produced under all conditions—both in a closed space and under the open sky. As he reduced the use of props, costumes, make-up, the artificial sound devices and projectors, his theatre became portable. It could be carried out anywhere. Instead of waiting for the spectators, he used to take his productions to where the masses were—in public parks, railway platforms, fields, in front of the factory gates, offices, college premises, and by the side of a busy road. Such productions neither demanded investment for the performance nor expected any income from the audience. So, the Third Theatre proved itself totally inexpensive and, therefore, "free". It is for this reason that his theatre comes to be recognized as the "Free Theatre", the "Intimate Theatre" and/or the "Alternative Theatre".

The plays *Procession, Bhoma,* and *Stale News* are written specially for the Third Theatre. The performances of these plays are arranged widely in'the widest possible range of situations and environments not only by Sircar's own group "Satabdi" but other theatre groups also. The earlier plays *Evam Indrajit, Baki Itihas, Tringsha Shatabdi,* and *Shesh Nei* are grouped together and called "Calcutta quartet" while the later plays *Procession, Indian History Made Easy, Bhoma, Stale News,* etc., may be grouped and named as the "colonialism quartet".

The successful performance of *Spartacus* at the Surendranath Park enabled Sircar to realize that now his theatre becomes flexible enough to be taken anywhere and at any time. Other plays in the "Satabdi" group, were also performed later in villages with great success. Their acceptance at the village proved the vigour and vitality of the Third Theatre. The "Satabdi" resumed giving open air performances at public parks, villages, and other places while it continued using the hall for their regular weekly performances.

Repeated visits to the villages of India made Sircar and his team conscious of the problems of the real India. This experience is reflected in his plays. His plays have been produced in various Indian languages such as Hindi, English, Marathi, etc. In May 1978, Satabdi was invited to Bangalore to present four plays. The response received there gives Sircar a confidence that the Third Theatre may soon develop at a number of places in Karnataka. Observing the overwhelming response to the plays at various states, Sircar comes to the conclusion, "Slowly but surely the Third Theatre is taking root in the soil of India." (Sircar, *On* 52)

Sircar's theatre started serving two purposes, moving in two different directions: first, an intimate theatre where an intense emotional communication is possible, and second, a theatre which can go to where the people are—without waiting for them to come to a specified place.

As the second form of the Third Theatre was similar to the already prevalent Street Theatre, the spectators could not differentiate it from the Street Theatre. The upshot of it was that Sircar's theatre is hailed as the Street Theatre or a variation of the Street Theatre. However, Subhedu Sarkar points out the distinction between the Street Theatre and Third Theatre. He states:

> Sircar never imposes his views on spectators like the playwright of street corner plays. His real intention, it seems, is to expose the contradictions of society and urge people to take note of their responsibilities. Whereas the goal of agitational street-corner plays is to move audiences emotionally and persuade them to vote for the Left, Sircar remains satisfied by appealing to their judgement. (Sarkar xxxv-xxxvi)

Sircar wants that each of his play has to take people on a ride. It is a journey into one's self from a stance outside one's own cultured viewpoint. His art aims at liberating us from our "cribbed, cabined, and confined" existence and helps us become, in one word, "human"—as human as possible.

Works Cited

Dass, Veena Noble. "Experiment and Innovation in Modern Indian Drama in Translation: The Plays of Mohan Rakesh, Badal Sircar, Vijay Tendulkar, and Girish Karnad." *Contemporary Indian Drama,* edited by Sudhakar Pandey and Freya Taraporwala, Prestige, 1990.

Dubey, Satyadev. Introduction. *Three Modern Indian Plays.* OUP, 1989.

Dutta, Ella. Introduction. *Three Plays*, by Badal Sircar, Seagull, 2009.

Sarkar, Subhendu. Introduction. *Two Plays: Indian History Made Easy, Life of Bagala*, by Badal Sircar, OUP, 2010.

Sircar, Badal. *On Theatre.* Seagull, 2009.

———. *The Third Theatre.* Seagull, 1978.

9

Procession: Search for a Real Home

Introduction

Nobody can understand Calcutta, the incorrigible, the impossible, summertime. One hundred and nine degrees Fahrenheit in the shade. A Procession.

So observed the noted economist Ashok Mitra in his brilliant article, "Calcutta Every Day" published in *Economic and Political Weekly*, Mumbai, 1969 (Mitra 6). Since the eighteenth century, Calcutta is considered to be the city of processions. "Everybody of the year, we can see hundreds, and more often thousands of people converge in processions across the wide and not-so-wide thorough-fares of Calcutta and shouting their heads off. Processions all around the year, sun or shower. It is a daily French Revolution-bloodless, colourful processions. Processions full of words and sounds." (Bhattacharjee 114)

For a long time, Sircar had in mind the idea of making a kind of montage on Calcutta. He found in a collage of slogans from the Calcutta processions "aural images of the religions, social and political emotions of the people of the city" (Bandyopadhyay 167). About the production of the play, Sircar writes:

> It is one of the very few plays where I had the idea of the production even before I began writing it, particularly, the procession idea. (Qtd. by Ella 5)

Sircar used to go to Anganmanch early on Sundays to arrange the seats in a way that streets and lanes were worked inside the audience. He did it to see whether the idea would work or not, and then, satisfied with his scheme of open stage, he began to write the play *Procession*.

For Sircar, Calcutta is an artificial city, created in the colonial interest of a foreign nation. It appears to him as "a city of alien culture based on English education, repressing, disturbing, buying, and promoting for sale the real culture of the country" (Sircar, "Letter" 5). Therefore, the social life in Calcutta has come to reflect the operation of the dual phenomenon of reconciliation/adjustment and conflict/confrontation. The unemployed angry youth, human degradation, pavement dwellers, pestering beggars, etc., have been the problem of the city in the pre- as well as post-colonial period. The stress and strain of living is unbearable; poverty and distress are writ large on the face of the city. In striking contrast stand a posh area of sophisticated people with rows of splendid buildings, spacious roads and glittering lights.

On the one side of the picture, there is the absence of gainful means of livelihood and on the other, there are the rich and affluent people, enjoying themselves with the advents of colonial period. This disparity gradually leads to an erosion of values. People follow any flag, bash any head if they are offered money. For this reason, the renowned poet-essayist Buddhadev Bose found Calcutta to be "complex, tossed in self-contradictions, and dazzling in beauty" (Qtd. in Shampa 120). And to Satyajit Ray, it appeared as "a monstrous, teeming, and bewildering city." (Qtd. in Shampa 120)

And politically speaking, Calcutta is considered to be one of the most sensitive cities in the world. It is a city towards which the other countries in the world have the mixed feelings of hope and fear. In a sense, Calcutta, as pointed out by Nishith Ranjan, is "both a lesson and a warning to India, a challenge and a question mark." (N. Ray 110)

The American social scientist Geoffrey Moorhouse states about Calcutta:

> ...The story of Calcutta is the story of India and the story of the so-called third world in miniature. It is the story of how and why Empire was created and what

> happened when Empire finished. It is the story of the people turning violently to communism for salvation. It is also the story of Industrial Revolution. The imperial residues of Calcutta, a generation after Empire ended, is both monstrous and a marvellous city. (Moorhouse; qtd. in N. Ray 110)

The play *Procession* is an authentic montage on this monstrous and marvellous city of Calcutta which addresses itself to the condition of the third world countries despite its strong Calcutta-oriented origin and urbane appeal. That is why this play could go like "a wave all over the country and on to Pakistan also" (Hashmi 145). Written to meet the demands of the Third Theatre movement, it has come to be a very popular street play. It has earned the distinction of being the most translated and the most performed of Sircar's later plays. It was first performed on April 14, 1974 at the village Ramachandrapur, West Bengal. Originally, the play is written in Bengali. It was performed by the Satabdi and was directed by the playwright himself. Sadanand Menon opines: "This play could contribute to the growth of a standard of political theatre quite unique in our country in the seventies." (Menon 10)

Sircar is attached to the city of Calcutta in more than one way and has an intimate feel of the urban consciousness of this city. He has a profound understanding of the middle-class life and, through almost all his major plays, he is found probing into the Calcutta middle-class mind. For this reason, his four plays, *Evam Indrajit*, *Baki Itihas*, *Tringsha Shatabdi* and *Shesh Nei* have been grouped together and called Calcutta quartet.

The Structure of the Play

Procession is a play "that causes the Third Theatre techniques to be adapted even by conventional directors" (Sircar, Interview; qtd. in Sen 75). At the very beginning of the play, Sircar makes it clear: "*Procession* is not meant to be performed on the proscenium stage. It has to be staged in an open space with the audience, seated all around it, or on the floor of a hall. If performed indoors, the chairs and backless benches for the audience should be so arranged as to suggest a maze, with a road going in knots and rounds. The road will constitute the acting area, with the audience sitting on both sides, the way people stand on both sides of a street to watch a procession passing. The actors will have two entrances or exits" (13). Sircar offers a diagrammatical representation of the stage as indicated below:

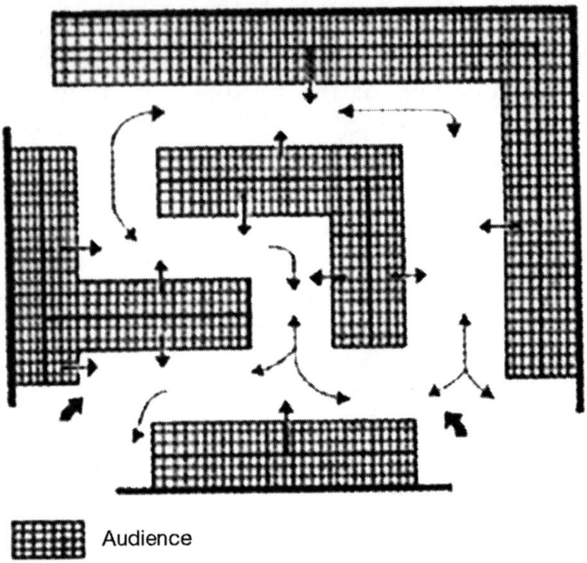

Out in the open, the first sequence is usually dropped. The play opens with Khoka entering the acting area, coming to the centre, dropping dead with a scream and the Chorus bursting in immediately with 'What's that? What's that?' and spreading all over the acting area. Later on, actors enact being obstructed at bends and crossing to convey the sense of an intricate maze of roads and routes criss-crossing all through. (13)

Bharucha, who witnessed a performance of the play comments: "Sircar creates the most bewildering environment with the bodies, backs, faces and profiles of the spectators. When the actors begin to move between and around the environment created by the spectators, the effect is starting: one can almost see a procession winding its way around the streets of Calcutta." (Bharucha 157)

Procession is Sircar's one of the most intricately structured plays. It comprises innumerable transitions and juxtapositions. The 'actors' are found,moving constantly in accordance with the relentless flow of events presented in the play. Khoka is lost "searching through roads and roads, processions and processions" (36). He has no longer any belief in processions. All processions, for him are: "death processions! Only—death!" (47) Every day in the streets, in the streams of masses,....he is dying. He is being killed. So, he says: "I'll be killed tomorrow. Day after,...next week. Next month. Next year...." (17)

As the play develops, Khoka continues to be killed by various tensions and every day calamities of the life of Calcutta. In contrast with this, the Old Man is in the search of something. He has been searching since his childhood, that is, when he was Khoka. He is delineated being interested and fascinated to see "the new road...beyond the bend" (19). And through processions and processions, he sought the road to his home, "not the old home, other home, true home, truly true home" (27). He has lost his way several times. Actually, seeking through roads and processions, he has become old. But he is not tired of walking and searching.

As the Old Man searches for the "true procession", the member of the Chorus enter the performing area now and then and, shout and mime, suggesting scenes depicting different facets of life in Calcutta. First, they shout headlines from various newspapers, the black marketing of essential commodities, the breakdown in railway schedules, and the postponement of examinations (11-12). This sequence is juxtaposed with the most effective evocation of sounds in a railway station. Hawkers, salesmen, and beggars vie with one another to attract the attention of the people. The playwright also describes the entry and exit of the passengers and standing on the toes of the previous ones. In the words of Nishith Ranjan Ray "The Calcuttans have literally mastered the art of living dangerously, for living depends on movements to and from places of work" (N. Ray 103). While they commute, they shout, argue, and fight.

Sircar alternates the nationalist slogan of "*Vande Mataram*" (30) (Hail Mother) with the religious cry of the Muslims, "*Alla*

Ho Akbar!" (30) (God is Great). This alternation precipitates the communal riot instantly (R. Jagannathan 9). The performers fight, collapse, rise and join in a slow, tired walk forming a procession of refugees (31) when five of the Chorus join in the singing of "*Saare Jehaan se achha Hindustan hamara*" (My Hindustan, the best of all the lands...) (31) one of the most popular songs of the Indian Freedom Movement, the one by Prof. Iqbal.

In the next sequence, the essential hollowness of the Indian patriotism is exposed more explicitly when a caricature of the ruling class, that is, the Master comes in and calls upon each of the persons in the Chorus to move on and make his way along the route. He spouts pious platitudes.

Remember our national heritage...numberless martyrs in our struggle for freedom...the invincible strength of the principle of non-violence...it is our responsibility to give spiritual leadership to the world. Remember the greatness of democracy in India... the fundamental rights of the Constitution. Remember the Green Revolution, the Nationalization of Banks, Family Planning, Dollar aid, the nuclear blast, MISA arrests. (31-32)

Bharucha found that the preposterous juxtapositions of "the Dollar aid" (an imaginary scheme) MISA (a repressive law, passed by Indira Gandhi during the Emergency) and the Indian "democracy" amused the audience. (Bharucha 160)

The political satire continues in the following sequence that depicts the preparation of an election campaign. The Chorus in the play represents the majority of people in Calcutta who continue to accept the corruption that pervades their lives. They look to the ruling class for advice and help. The master preaches them that communism is the greatest enemy of civilization and that it is the religion of the animals. When they cry that they are dying, the Master "enlightens" them with his assurance that "There's heaven for you after you die.... Animals have no heaven" (35). However, this blessing does not bring about any change in their plight. They continue to suffer from unemployment, factory lockouts and, the poverty that prevents most of them from getting married or paying the doctor's bills

(35). The master, on hearing their problems, offers them a bottle of liquor calling it "Nectar. To help you forget" (36). The old man also joins them, calling liquor "the comic relief" and the only bit "of humour in this *duniya's* deadly dull drama" (36). But still he is optimistic as he goes on seeking:

> I need to know now where *this* way is going.... First, the right side of the road chasing you, then the left...from now on I've got to fix my north and south.... (37)

Here, the directions 'left' and 'right' symbolize the leftist movement and right wing ideology. The common man is shown as under the influence of both at the same time.

Khoka's informing the audience that he has been killed and the Old Man's constant assurance that he has simply lost his way—are used at regular interval as refrains. Sircar juxtaposes here the fact and the optimism or reality and illusion.

Sircar criticizes the middle class mentality to remain indifferent to the plight of the poor. Rustom Bharucha opines that such indifference of the middle class to the plight of the poor strengthens the power of reactionary governments (Bharucha 162). When the Chorus sings, "It's the best of all lands and the land of my birth" (44). Khoka runs in shouting "Stop it! Stop these lies! It's not the truth!... An attempt to confuse you? I have been killed, I am killed every day, I will be killed every day—that's the truth!" '(44)

The Officer who is the representative of the ruling class shuts his mouth. Throughout the play, he is always seen repeating his familiar lines. "Nobody's murdered. Nobody's lost. Everything's in order" (28). "Go home!" (17) Through his constant assurance, he wants to give a message that life in Calcutta is normal. The juxtaposition of the howls and the assurance by the Officer and the Master is one of the most outrageous instances of Sircar's political satire.

In the end, there is a frantic sequence where the Chorus members raise slogans from a multitude of processions. Khoka runs in screaming that all the slogans are lies, and that he does not believe in their processions, and their rhetoric. Confronting the audience, he shouts out in despair:

> You sit on the sidelines watching processions.... Silently you watch the killings.... We are killers, all. We all kill, we all get killed.... Stop it. Stop it— (47-48)

The Officer seizes Khoka. He is assisted by the members of the Chorus. They take Khoka to different points in the space and kill him in different ways by beheading him, hanging him, firing a machine gun at him, by putting him into a gas chamber. At the end, the officer and the Chorus turn into a bomber aircraft pouring bombs on Khoka. The lights go out as Khoka's death-scream rends the darkness. (48)

However, the play ends on an optimistic note. The old man suddenly hears the music of the "true procession"—"the procession to show us a way. The way home"... (52). It is the procession of men. As he speaks, the Chorus comes in as a procession accompanied by music. The song without words follows then. "It is a song of hope, a song for the future. It is a procession of dreams. A song of dreams—Dreams that the Old Man and Khoka have dreamt. The people in the procession are holding hands. Old man holds Khoka's hand and leads him up to the procession and finally they become part of it.... The audience is invited to join. The procession continues" (53). The play ends by "rousing them from being the passive audience into active participants." (Sastri; qtd. in Shampa 149)

Thus, the play *Procession* strikes a note of hope in the end. In the words of Bharucha, "The spectators and actors intermingle and the entire space...becomes a swirling mass of humanity. It is one of those moments in the theatre when one becomes acutely aware of the possibilities of life and the essential brotherhood of man. Transcending the immediate issues of the play, it lingers long after the play ceases, compelling the spectators to re-examine their affinities and responsibilities as member of a society." (Bharucha 163)

Critical Interpretation and Appraisal of the Play

The play *Procession* is a continuation of the earlier play *Evam Indrajit* which is also about the 'residue' of the city of Calcutta middle-classes who have failed to adjust and got enmeshed in the day-to-day struggle for survival. But Indrajit is a serious, iconoclastic, angry, young man. Through him, the playwright depicts "the predicament of the middle class alienated man in an amoral, soulless society" (Raha 144). This unusual young man is finally reminded of his destiny by the writer, a commentator on the play's events and characters.

> Writer: We are the cursed spirits of Sisyphus. We have to push the rock to on the top-even if it just rolls down.
>
> ....
>
> Indrajit: Must we still live?
>
> ...
>
> Writer: We know no sacred places. Yet we must go on with the pilgrimage.... There's no respite. (59-60)

In the same way the Old Man in *Procession* tells Khoka:

> Old Man: The procession to show us way. The way home.
>
> Khoka: (tired) I've seen so many processions. They never show you the way. It's always the same road, the same.... (52)

Thus, the theme of *Evam Indrajit* is taken up or extended in *Procession* with a variation. Khoka is Indrajit's alter ego and the Old Man performs the same role as that of the Writer. Indrajit says: "...It won't ever get completed. Its end is its beginning" (Act III. p. 59). And its (*Evam Indrajit*) end has found a new beginning in the subsequent play *Procession.* It is like a circle, where the beginning and the end merge into each other.

Like *Evam Indrajit, Procession* too has no beginning or end. Khoka or anyone else in the play is not tied up in a plot. Actually, there is no plot, no theme at all. There are no 'Acts' to 'control' Khoka and others. They are more unconventional and free than Indrajit. "Khoka and others are not 'characters' at all—or 'characters of any consistency'—or 'individualized characters'" (Bhattacharjee 128). So, the characters are the prototypes of particular classes in a society at a particular time. Therefore, Khoka is the prototype of the dejected middle-class youth of the early seventies. And, there is no protagonist. The spectator is supposed to assume the role of a protagonist in the play, "making the theatrical incident experimental, indeterminate and open-ended." (Dass 69)

The script of the play is of a non-verbal nature. Sircar has made an effective use of pantomime or to use the more recent term body language. Silence and gesture speak more effectively than words. According to Samik Bandyopadhyay, "The idiom of the slogans chosen, lends itself naturally to the technique of verbal repetition, the continuous and ironic reiteration of a limited score of words and phrases, that has been a common feature of the dramaturgy of the non-proscenium, non-verbal theatre" (Bandyopadhyay 167). Actually, what Sircar wishes to communicate through this play are the clear-cut facts and concrete truths about the happenings in Calcutta.

To quote Ella Dutta again, "*Procession*, the most translated and the most performed of his (Sircar) later plays, is considered by many to have a universal appeal despite its strong Calcutta-oriented origin its urban sensibility.... The play was well received even in the villages where the image of Khoka's repeated death is not an abstract idea, distantly removed to the experiences of the urban middle-class." (Dutta 5-6)

It is a play about a situation. As it is related to the various processions that people form for their legitimate demands, it cannot be performed in a theatre. It has to be performed in an open space with the road, through which the processions, that indicate man's consciousness, will go along their ways. Such events in the play, naturally, intertwine themselves around the islands of seating spaces for the audience. The play invites the active-participation of the audience to join the symbolic procession, the real procession of real men that will "show us a way. The way home." (52)

The play has several messages. It throws light on the violence and corruption that erupt in the post-colonial world. It is Sircar's comment on the political situation in India. It is about the angry, frustrated 1960 generation in search of home. It explores the impact of apathy, indifference and lovelessness on human life. According to Sarbani Sen "The theme and message of the play is unmistakable. It speaks of lost generations where people got lost. They can only follow. It is also about violence and corruption in post-colonial India. It narrates how "I am killed every day. Every day, killed, every day, dead, every day. I'll be killed tomorrow" (17). The play using repetition chorus, and montage techniques might be making a political statement, but no red flags, jargon or propaganda cloud its horizon. The play highlights the soullessness of modern religion and politics and the endless crowds, continuous agitations, serpentine queues and senseless rush of contemporary Indian life. True to the Indian traditions of complete theatre, "Sircar uses haunting music, familiar rhymes, earthy metaphors and traditional symbols" (Sen 75-76). It brings to notice that there is something more in the play than sheer ruthlessness, lovelessness, murder, and bloodshed. There are poetry, humour and irony, and wit also.

The play demands a serious attention of the audience as it has a tremendous pace. Scenes change, events happen at breakneck speed. It is rather different in nature since it anticipates the responses and participation of the audience. So, it stops suddenly in the middle of fast action expecting the audience to ponder over the situation. In this sense, it is Sircar's sincere effort to bring about a change in the mind-set of the people and thereby in the society at large.

In "Voyages in the Theatre", Sircar notes down his experience about the first performance of *Procession*. He writes: "There was pin-drop silence and rapt attention during the whole one-hour performance. At the end of the play, we sing a wordless melody, holding hands, and invite the audience to join us. An old Santhal came up with tears in his eyes and instead of holding hands, he embraced the actor. This old Santhal, the man who walked miles with us, the beggar woman who contributed the five-paise coin, the field labourer in Rangabelia village, these are the people we try to think about when our voyages tend to become hazardous and frustrating." (Sircar, *On* 116-17)

Before the performance of the play, Sircar has a little fear in mind whether the play can be understood and appreciated by the villagers. Out of 300 audiences, nearly 250 were barefooted, bare-bodied Santhals. The only thing that appeared positive and supportive to the playwright was that all of them (Santhals) knew Bengali.

"How can we get across?—(That) was our thought. The play has no story, no character and it is full of city images. And then, suddenly, I had the realization that there is nothing in the play that could be difficult for them to understand. Rather, they would probably understand it better, for the young man getting killed everyday is a concrete experience for them, not abstract as in our case. And the old home that the Old Man refuses to return to is nothing but the present society, and the new home he is seeking is a place where there will be no hunger, no privation, and no injustice." (Sircar, *On* 116)

In *Procession,* Sircar exposes the decadence and degradation of human beings in civilization. The play is a collage of diverse episodes taken from the day-to-day life of middle-class man. The heterogeneous events and incidents communicate the same theme of 'being lost' in the so-called civilized society. So, the play communicates an underlying unity of theme behind the rich diversity of events and episodes. The characters are not types. They are just representative and symbolic. The Old Man represents Sircar's optimism; Khoka is the victim of the civilized society. The city of Calcutta stands for civilization for which the Officer and the Master are the custodians. Khoka and the Old Man form one group and the Officer and the Master, another. These two groups are antagonistic and show the victim-victimizer relationship which characterizes all societies in all ages. The old Man is always in search of 'home' and Khoka is constantly haunted with the feeling of being killed. The people, that is, the Chorus in the play blindly follow the order of the Officer and the Master to start the procession since they believe that civilization does not exist without masters.

The Officer's indifference to Khoka at the very beginning of the play, when the latter tries to inform him that he is killed everyday, "shows how the perception of the reality is completely discouraged with (sic by the) oppressive forces." (Babu 102)

The first procession in the play is a funeral procession. The playwright gives the list of various processions through the

Old Man who encourages the people to join the procession: "Michhils for food and clothes, Michhils for salvation. Michhils for the revolution, military Michhils, Michhils of refugees, Michhils for flood relief,..." (18). In Translator's "Afterword", Samik Bandyopadhyay states: "There are waves through the play *Procession* of these different movements, in time sequences located in history. In the sequence..., one can read the history of the anti-colonial freedom movement, from the early fervour of nationalism registered in the patriotic songs to the pro-imperialist reaction, from terrorism to Gandhian non-violence, to the rise of communalism, leading to the Partition of the country and to the migration of refugees." (Bandyopadhyay 167)

As the play progresses, the various processions are acted. The revolutionary processions reflect Sircar's disillusionment with the existing communist parties and their movements. Sircar's main object is to raise the consciousness and create awareness of the issues. For it, one has to read between the lines. Sircar is a social reformer who wants to bring about a silent, gradual change in people's attitude towards life and its problems. So, the play is, as usual, thought-provoking. It evokes a note of protest in the minds of audience.

The character of Khoka in the play is the representative of the suffering figure in the civilized society. The Old Man's information that Khoka is not lost; he comes back home, the real home but not the old one, has various connotations. Here Khoka symbolizes a child who is not spoiled by civilization; one who still possesses humanity. The old home is the contemporary society which is replete with inequality, exploitation, corruption, degradation and dehumanization. The new home stands for the future society, based on such values as equality, fraternity, and humanity. Sircar dreams of that new home. One can find the reflection of the home in his next play *Beyond the Land of Hattamala*. The play is Sircar's indictment of the myth of nationalism. However, what he criticizes is not an individual, a class or any government but the system. "The Old Man's search for the real road to the real home symbolizes the search of mankind for the right way to regain their lost paradise, the primal bliss." (Babu 107)

In a nutshell, it can be stated that "the play raises a collective voice against the ruthless system. It gives a hope to those who want to survive by joining the mainstream of the procession towards freedom" (Bhattacharjee 155). The last procession, depicted in the play is a human procession where all human beings, sinking their differences of caste, religion and nation, are united and where they collectively endeavour to solve all their problems and try to create emotionally refined, integrated and conscious world "where tireless striving stretches its arms towards perfection." (Tagore 33)

Works Cited

Babu, Manchi Sarat. *Indian Drama Today: Study in the Theme of Cultural Deformity*. Prestige, 1997.

Bandyopadhyay, Samik. Afterward. *Three Plays*, by Badal Sircar, Seagull, 2009.

Bhattacharjee, Shampa. *Badal Sircar's Street Plays: A Thematic Study*. An M. Phil. Dissertation. Submitted to Kakatiya University, Warangal. Feb. 1994.

Bharucha, Rustom. *Rehearsals of Revolution: The Political Theatre of Bengal*. Seagull Books, 1983.

Bose, Buddhadev. Quoted in Shampa Bhattacharjee.

Dass, Veena Noble. "Experiment and Innovation in Modern Indian Drama in Translation: The Plays of Mohan Rakesh, Badal Sircar, Vijay Tendulkar, and Girish Karnad." *Contemporary Indian Drama*, edited by Sudhakar Pandey and Freya Taraporwala, Prestige, 1990.

Dutta, Ella. Introduction. *Three Plays*, by Badal Sircar, Seagull, 2009.

Hashmi, Safdar. *The Right to Perform*. Sahmat, 1989.

Menon, Sadanand. "Towards a People Theatre." *The Sunday Observer*, Sept. 30, 1984.

Mitra, Ashok. *Calcutta Diary*. (Collection of Essays previously published in *Economic and Political Weekly* during 1968-75.) Frank Cass, 1976.

Moorhouse, Geoffrey, quoted in Nishith Ranjan Ray.

Raha, Kironmoy. *Bengali Theatre*. Delhi: National Book Trust, 1978.

R. Jagannathan, "Banning of Processions in Unfortunate." *Indian Express*, Sept. 20, 1993.

Ray, Nishith Ranjan. *Calcutta: A Profile of a City*. K.P. Bachi, 1986.

Sastri, I. Sircar. *Enact*, July.-Aug. 1978/1981. N.P.

Sen, Sarbani. "What's New about New Theatre?—A Comparative Study of Badal Sircar's *Procession* with Wole Soyinka's *The Road as Post-Colonial Theatre.*" *New Directions in Indian Theatre*, editors Sudhakar Pandey and Freya Barua, Prestige, 1994.

Sircar, Badal. "A Letter from Badal Sircar." *The Drama Review*. (US), Vol. 26, No. 2, Summer 1982.

———. Personal Interview, quoted in Sarbani Sen.

———. *On Theatre*. Seagull, 2009.

Tagore, Rabindranath. "Where the Mind is without Fear." *Gitanjali*. Macmillan, 2004.

(N.B. All textual quotations are from Sircar, Badal. *Three Plays*. Seagull, 2009.)

10

Bhoma: Cutting down the Poisonous Trees

Introduction

Badal Sircar is an Indian playwright of international repute. He is an extraordinary committed artist who views his theatre as a form of social work. He is the founder director of the most inventive Bengali theatre group "Satabdi", and directed plays for the conventional stage during the fifties and sixties before pioneering his Third Theatre which aims at awakening the urban audience to the exploitation and the rural audience to a sense of its power. So, "He is", according to Rustom Bharucha, "the only director in the contemporary Bengali theatre who is capable of creating a genuine people's theatre—a theatre supported and created by the people and not merely performed for the people" (Bharucha 188). Sircar makes the society, specially the middle-class one, feel guilty for being indifferent towards man and his problems. His plays express his anguish at the prevailing social condition and the role man has to play in these conditions.

The play *Bhoma* explores the paradox of the co-existence of large food surpluses and widespread hunger and malnutrition in many third world countries. "After independence, the inventions and modernization in agricultural field have given rise to an expected surplus which by the end of the 1970s reached the fantastic figure of 20 million tonnes of grain. Still poverty (and malnutrition) continued and hundreds of millions of Indians were unable to meet minimum daily calorie requirements...." (Bhattacharjee 158)

Bhoma illuminates the contradictions and disparities of the socio-economic situations in contemporary society. The play is totally different in its approach to the act of playwriting. It is based on the actual experiences that Badal Sircar had while working in Rangabelia, an area in the Sundarbans as a city planner with the Comprehensive Area Development Cooperation (CADC). This direct exposure to the rural areas develops certain social attitudes in Sircar's mind which find expression in his plays. He is of the opinion "that unless there is rural development, unless economic planning is linked with town planning, the whole exercise is useless. And that the Calcutta Municipal Development Authority concept (CMDA) is all wrong." (Dutta 7)

The play depicts the impact of lovelessness on our society. Sircar seems to believe in the absurd philosophy that human life is essentially irrational, illogical, out of harmony the result of which is the chronic state of uncertainty, anguish and depression. There is no plot, no characterization, no story, no continuity; nothing actually happens on the stage. The playwright allows the absurd, the illogical, and the irrational to happen on stage to bring about the central concern that this is the true nature of human life. "Whatever there is to say, the actors say directly to the audience through words, sounds and their whole body." (Sircar, Preface 57)

The Structure of the Play

The play is the outcome of Sircar's conversation with Tushar Kanjilal, the headmaster of Rangabelia Village School. In the Preface, he writes about the evolution of the play:

> But Bhoma's story is not there in this play. Seeing, feeling and learning about our surroundings shock us, hurt us, anger us—these have come out in disjoined, dramatic pictures. Bhoma's pictures was then part of those pieces. But when those pictures were strung together into a play then somehow it was Bhoma's image which started to become the link and at the end the play could not be called anything but *Bhoma.* (Sircar, Preface 57)

The first performance of the play took place on 21st March 1976 at village Rangabelia, West Bengal, in India. Originally, it was written in Bengali. It was performed by the "Satabdi" with six actors and was directed by the playwright himself. Sircar says: *Bhoma* is not a play aiming to entertain the well-dressed front row audiences in a lush theatre. I am sure that those who do that kind of theatre will not touch my play anyway." (Sircar, Preface 58)

The action of the play begins with an evocation of the rural life with six actors wearing identical dress. Some actors pose as trees and two of the actors turn into wood-cutters felling trees. In the paddy fields, some actors plough, sow seeds and harvest while others form into a machine. The rhythms and sounds of the machine in the background suggest the proximity of urban development.

The play is absurd in nature. It is noticed from the very beginning. The characters have no names. Instead, they have numbers such as ONE, TWO, etc. ONE goes on searching for Bhoma while THREE speaks of love. Bhoma is not a character yet his presence is felt throughout the play. Bhoma symbolizes various roles. He grows from a poor peasant into a powerful image. There is a discussion about the evolution:

TWO: The blood of fish is cold.

ONE: The blood of man is also cold.

THREE: No. The blood of man is warm.

ONE: It was. Before. Now it's cold. Theory of Evolution. Darwin.

Had man's blood not grown cold, he wouldn't have survived.

THREE: What would he have done then?

ONE: Died. Before extinct, like the dinosaurs.

THREE: The blood of the dinosaurs. Was it cold or warm?

ONE: I don't know. (60)

The arguments lack coherence. It is not scientific but it symbolizes that human beings, like dinosaurs, will vanish in future if they continue to be loveless and apathetic. The word "cold" has an eerie resonance as it is repeated by the actors in the refrain. It is through this repetition that Sircar reinforces his views concerning the indifference of man to man. One is grieved to see or hear "what man has made of man," in the words of Wordsworth.

TWO talks about his job, his family and his problems. THREE feels bored and shouts at him to stop talking. But he talks about his love for a girl while others laugh at him. Then, their attention shifts to tourism and urban development.

FOUR: Television! Television! It's here now. Don't worry!

FIVE: Metro Rail! Flyovers! The Second Hooghly Bridge! Don't worry. (63)

One brings to notice the need of developing the rural area: "But seventy-five percent of India's population live in villages, not in cities." TWO, FIVE, SIX sing a song composed by Tagore which describes villages beautifully while FOUR speaks about the special welfare programmes of villages that is given great publicity on the radio.

Then a group of businessmen performs a dance of greed on the stage. It is interrupted by ONE who calls "Bhoma-a-a!" (64) aloud. To the repeated question "What's that? (64) he narrates "Bhoma is the forest. Bhoma is the paddy field. Bhoma is the village." (64)

Eighty percent of people in India live in villages. The villagers have to provide good food grains for all the people. The development of nation lies in the progress of the villages. But the peasants are not supplied with water, seeds and fertilizers. Most of them have no sufficient land. They are so poor that they cannot afford fertilizers and water pumps sets for their small-sized lands. The families, which have no land at all, work on other people's lands as hired labourers. They live on daily wages and get four rupees a day. Theirs is a poor family with five to ten dependents. With their meagre earnings they cannot afford to buy rice; so, they buy wheat but not enough for chapattis. However, they can afford porridge of it just with water and salt. But they are even deprived of this work in summer and have to go starved or half-starved.

The whole country is divided into the two large sections—rural and urban. The urban middle-class people remain indifferent to the pathetic condition of the poor villagers. They are conscious of their comforts and want more and more facilities for their city which will render the villages poorer and poorer. For the development of city, the investment of billions of rupees is needed. While a few million rupees is enough for the irrigation of a few thousand acres of land in villages. The ultimate result of this investment is that all the 3,000 acres of land will yield gold! (68) The attention is diverted by the talk about the development of the city.

TWO: The Second-Hoogly bridge—only 600 million rupees.

THREE: Digging in Calcutta for better streets and better sewers—only 2,000 million rupees spent so far.

FOUR: The Metro Rail will cost only 3000 million rupees. (69)

In comparison with this amount, the farmers need a small amount on loan at the usual bank rate. They are ready to repay the whole amount with interest on harvest. The result of it is that the land will yield gold; the farm labourers will have to work throughout the year and will get higher wages. But no one is ready to take the cognizance of it. This throws light on the exploitation of millions of villages by a few cities. In Preface to *Three Plays*, Ella Dutta points out Sircar's aim of writing plays. She rightly observes: "What he wishes to communicate through his theatre are clear cut facts, concrete truths about what is happening in villages, the nature of exploitation both industrial and agricultural, the urban stranglehold on the rural economy. He feels that his first mission is to make people aware." (Dutta 4)

Exploitation of the weaker by the stronger is the characteristic feature of all societies in all ages. The villages are exploited by the cities. Within villages, the landlords exploit the poor peasants, while in cities industrialists exploit labourers. It is illustrated through the example of two companies named Mahamaya Engineering Company and Samson and Blackbird Company. Mahamaya Engineering Company is a small company which manufactures diesel pump sets for Samson and Blackbird Company. However, they stick the nameplate of Samson and Blackbird Company on the readymade set. They even prepare the specification literature for them, and supply it printed and ready. For each set, they get just ₹ 2,500. But even that is not paid in cash. The same set is sold for ₹ 4,625 by the Samson and Blackbird Company. Mahamaya Engineering Company gets its money only after the sets are sold. The upshot of it is that the Mahamaya Engineering Company always suffers from the shortage of capital to make new sets. So, they approach the manager of a bank for loan. The manager demands guarantees which the Mahamaya Engineering Company fails to give. So, the manager refuses to sanction the loan of a few thousand rupees to them but he readily sanctions Samson and Blackbird Company a big loan of one hundred and thirty thousand without security. Ultimately, the poor craftsman sell their Mahamaya Engineering Company for it is impossible for them to maintain the company without any capital.

The injustice of this situation is objectified in the narrative that follows. ONE and TWO speak of the predicament of a small farmer who needs a little amount of loan from the nationalized bank to buy some fertilizers and a diesel pump. He had already mortgaged his only property (an acre of land) to the moneylender and has nothing more to offer as security to the bank. So, he is denied the loan. He uses a pump set of the landlord Gadai Mitter and pays him at least ₹ 1,200 at the rate of seven rupees per hour for selling water to him. This cultivating paddy in the dry season for him is like "beggars craving to ride horses" (75). And, as he cannot use sufficient amount of good fertilizers and pests, he gets only less than eighteen quintals of paddy per acre against the expected yield of thirty quintals.

But Gadai Mitter who owns more than twenty-five acres of land and has a very costly pump set already is granted bank loan to buy again a Simbird pump set which he lends it to the poor peasants and makes money—easy money. Listening to all this FIVE shouts: "Nationalized banks in the service of agriculture!" (75) This is followed by the groaning of the poor farmers demanding water for cultivation.

> ONE: (groaning). We need water, give us water, we need water, give us water. We need water, give us water. (76)

This indicates that thousands of villagers have been affected by drought. The intensity of exploitation is expressed very effectively by exploiting the image of "blood". It is repeatedly conveyed that man's "blood" is getting cold. The playwright emphasizes it by using the technique of contrast.

> FIVE: It's a lie. In India men's blood boils, when Bloodthirsty Pakistan attacks India.
>
> THREE: When imperialist China attacks India!
>
> THREE: When the Indian cricket team loses a test match. (77)

As Bharucha notices, "This technique of accentuation, the significance of a statement by opposing it in one way or another, is constantly used by the playwright in *Bhoma*." (Bharucha 177)

The image blood has several connotations in the play. FIVE says, "Give me 'blood', I'll give you jobs... "Give me blood, I'll give you permits.... Give me blood, I'll give you kingdom" (77-78). "The word means 'money', 'murder' and 'sacrifice'. But it invariably implies exploitation and oppression. Sircar invigorates the image of "blood" step by step. The image is finally hurled at the urban middle class to make them feel remorseful for their apathy to the rural poor peasants" (Babu 132-33). Towards the end of the play, ONE says "There's the taste of Bhoma's blood on the tongue. We drink Bhoma's blood, and laugh and play. There's blood dripping down the sides of our mouths, dripping, dripping the poisonous plants are growing, growing. My blood, man's blood, becomes cold, c-o-l-d, c-o-l-d. (109)

The root-cause of this exploitation is lovelessness, indifference and isolation. Even the fine arts, which are considered to be the source of pleasure, also encourage the people to become loveless and thus indifferent to the suffering of the poor.

TWO: (in agony). Beggars and dogs fighting over left-overs from the wedding feast thrown out on the street.

ONE: Drown that noise with Ravi Shankar's sitar. (80)

Rat-race competition and individualism are also the causes of lovelessness. Material things become more valuable to people than human beings. Society is divided on the basis of religion, caste, class, etc. Religion which usually preaches love is converted into a loveless, materialistic institution.

Materialism has converted the homes into houses. Parents of middle-class families sell their property and borrow money to educate their children. Even the country also spends a great deal on their education. But being highly educated, they leave their parents and their country, in debts and serve abroad. This shows the exploitation of the developing countries by the developed ones. Sircar, here, criticizes the modern young generation that is ready to sell human values for the sake of money.

Materialism leads people to dishonesty and corruption. They do not have love for their motherland. The rulers exploit their nation and deposit their money in Switzerland. Ultimately, the country becomes more and more bankrupt while the rulers grow more and more affluent. However, through media, they try to present themselves as noble statesmen.

The worst consequence of lovelessness is the nuclear warfare. Atomic weapons not only destroy millions of people but also cause deformity to millions of children at several stages. Yet, people are not ready to pay attention to the deadly destructive power of nuclear weapons and feel very happy about their country's becoming a nuclear power. The solution of all these problems is collectivism and cooperation so that there will be the withdrawal of all egos (i.e., I) into a great unified 'we'.

Thus, the play exposes the effect of lovelessness on society which ultimately leads to the exploitation and oppression of peasants, workers, villages and developing countries by landlords, industrialists, cities and advanced countries. However, majority of the critics are of the opinion that the play focuses on the exploitation of the rural area by the urban one. According to K. Venkateswarlu, "*Bhoma* presents a vivid picture of the oppressed peasant by dramatizing a series of scenes in which he is socially oppressed and economically exploited" (Qtd. in Babu 136). The sterility, portrayed in the play, is similar to the one that we come across in T.S. Eliot's *The Waste Land.*

Throughout the play, it is not made clear who Bhoma is. However, it is observed that it is a very powerful symbol (representing "a common man" as a hero) that overpowers the talk which is related to corruption, exploitation and dehumanization. The refrain, "The "blood" of man is cold" reminds the audience what Eliot calls people "hollow men", the "stuffed men" who cannot raise the voice of protest. In the last part of the play, the actors try to search for Bhoma. It is told that it is necessary to find out Bhoma to change the world, to bring back love, to keep the "blood" warm. Bhoma is hungry. His mother is alive—sticking cow-dung cakes on the crumbling wall. Bhoma's father is seen putting up tattered sacks on his shack of mud and old tin. Bhoma's brother is found driving the herd of swines. The Bhomas come in groups after groups to Calcutta, stay in the suburbs of Sealdah, Tapsia, Dhapa, Kusumkumari, and on the pavements of Calcutta. Bhoma's mother, wife, sisters and daughters are seen washing pots and pans in the houses of the gentry, while "carrying in their wombs the children of the gentry..." (107). Bhoma is also there with "salt tears marking his torn check." (107)

Thus, Bhoma becomes a potent, meaningful symbol as the play progresses. He symbolizes the class of oppressed people. He is not just a poor peasant. He is a jungle. He is a cornfield. He is a village. He also symbolizes love, compassion and humanity. The root-cause of all problems is Bhoma's exploitation and the remedy for them lies in Bhoma's freedom. The play ends on an optimistic note:

ONE: This earth belongs to all of us, doesn't it Bhoma? If we all of us, could work our hardest to make

> everything we need and then all of us shared all we produced, then that queer picture that lets us buy up your "blood" to drink, the picture that you don't have and therefore can't get your rice—if we could destroy for ever that queer, obscene picture—I can't explain it, Bhoma! I can only understand if you don't rise up with your axe, then the forest of poisonous trees will never be cleared. (106)

Critical Interpretation and Appraisal of the Play

The play *Bhoma* is realistic in nature since it is based on the experiences Badal Sircar had while working in Rangabelia with the Comprehensive Area Development Corporation. About the production of the play, Sircar writes:

> *Bhoma* is a composition of many detached scenes that were written over a three-year period. Whenever I reacted strongly to a fact or a phenomenon I came across—in reality, in the newspaper, in a book, in a discussion—something emerged in the shape of a scene in a play. That is to say, there were speeches for actors but nothing on the left side of the colon to indicate the identity of the speaker of the lines. There were no dialogues as such, but connected speeches projected straight to the audience. When I wrote those scenes, I had no idea that I was creating a play—it was more like writing a diary. These scenes were read out to the group members.... The group began to deal with the scenes I wrote and with the contributions they made, the play *Bhoma* gradually emerged. (Sircar, *On* 117-18)

While working with the CADC in Rangebelia, Sircar observed that much of the agricultural land is owned by a small minority of surplus farmers and most of the rural population is landless, owing less than half an acre each or no land at all. Again, the small farmer is forced first to mortgage and then to sell his land for various reasons such as harvest failures, daughters' marriages, accidents, illness, etc. Each drought or flood creates many new landless. The farmers who lose their land, lose their only source of security and are forced to join the ranks of the rural poor, completing either for work as wage labourers or for land to cultivate on a share cropping basis. This is the picture of the rural area in our country.

The food problem is essentially a problem of poverty. Through Green Revolution, government tries to solve it by the introduction of new seeds, agricultural inputs and methods of production which will result in higher yields per acre. The key-problem is the distribution of the consequent gains. The poor are hungry because they do not have sufficient income. They will remain hungry as long as they lack the purchasing power, because food is produced for those who can afford to buy it. The basic cause of poverty in the countryside is the unequal distribution of land. While the privileged few enjoy various comforts, life for the average Indian villagers has been getting harder and harder.

The public food distribution system mainly benefits the minority of urban upper- and middle-class residents and the government employees. The rural poor are not the target of the distribution system. All the mess is there, because the country is run by urban people with urban interests and habits.

"West Bengal, being one of the states in India is not an exception. It is not "so golden" as it is described—as "Sonar Bangla". All the political parties, according to Luykx, shunned the rural poor there, at least up until the mid 1960s. And later, even the political parties stood to gain more political ground by promoting disaffection among the rural population than by prosecuting its cause." (Luykx 184)

In *Bhoma*, Badal Sircar depicts these burning issues in Bengal. The play exposes the spirit of the oppressed rural population against the backdrop of the glamour of the city of Calcutta. *Bhoma* is not entirely Sircar's creation since "Satabdi" has also created images out of their experience and feelings and they have been incorporated in the play.

The story of *Bhoma* is actually one of those scenes. Sircar heard the story from the headmaster of Rangabelia village school who had actually met Bhoma. At that time, he was 72.

Once, he has a fight with a tiger in which he lost an eye and gained a big hollow on his cheek.

> Bhoma gradually became more and more important in the play, to the extent of leading it his name but he did not appear as a character in the play, nor did his life-story figure in it. The play speaks not of Bhoma but of the Bhomas who constitute a phenomenon, a social reality. In the collection of loose and detached scenes dealing with subjects as diverse as the problem of groundwater, the hazards of nuclear tests...and so on, the connecting link is a city man in search of Bhoma, the only person who is capable of clearing the jungle of poisonous trees that our society has become, to make it habitable. (Sircar, *On* 118)

Thus, the play is the upshot of Sircar's involvement with Rangabelia. It was due to his work with CADC when he had direct exposure to the countryside. This close encounter develops certain social attitudes in his mind which find expression in his work. He narrates: "The Rangabelia experiences, Bhoma's story, the life-story of the wood-cutters in the forest, which we had all heard from the school teacher there—we separately wrote down our reactions to them.... 'I felt that the play would be a search for Bhoma by a man like me, by people like us.' Some images, also written down—the blood of fish, the blood of humans, cold blood and warm blood—worked themselves into different points of the play like refrains." (Dutta 6-7)

The arguments and events in the play have no continuity. But all of them reflect that the basic cause of poverty in society is exploitation, resulted out of lovelessness and lack of sympathy for fellow human beings. Throughout the play it is suggested that human beings, like dinosaurs, will become extinct if they continue to be loveless, apathetic and indifferent, since the blood of man is getting cold.

The intensity of exploitation is expressed very effectively by exploiting the image of blood. It is repeated in Sircar's another play in a different manner: blood has an advantage. "The rains wash it all away. Wash it into drains, from the drains to the rivers, from the rivers into the sea. Not many people know this—seawater has high blood content, and this is increasing every day" (Sircar, *Stale* 159). Man is interested in sucking the blood of his own fellow-being. That is why the playwright says: "Bhoma's blood, red blood, blossoms into white jasmines of rice on your plates. Twice every day." (95)

The play also criticizes the inventions of science such as atomic weapons. The countries feel proud of creating this powerful nuclear warfare. The nuclear tests pollute the environment because of radioactivity. They "have released enough radioactivity to cause the birth of the two million maimed and deformed children… (89). Still people are not ready to realize the destructive side of the nuclear weapons. Although they have the dreadful experience of Hiróshima, they think that nuclear power can be used for peaceful purpose. Sircar criticizes the complacency with the view: "Peace, Peaceful birth, Peaceful death" (89). In between the two—a peaceful, deformed life.

It is observed from the play that, in this so-called civilized, cultured and modern society, people are not only indifferent to the suffering of the poor but also loveless to one another. That is why ONE says: "My heart has dried up. My heart is a piece of leather. Can you spare me a drop of water to moisten it? TWO: Sorry go on" (92). Veena Noble Dass observes: "When Sircar came in contact with the villagers of the Sundarbans, he was shocked by the dehumanized condition of their life. But more than shocked he was enraged by the fact that the urban community of West Bengal could be so totally indifferent to the impoverishment of the villagers in the Sundarbans. The indifference is due to lovelessness.… Everybody needs and wants love but nobody is ready to love others." (Qtd. in Babu 136)

It seems that Sircar may have the dream of egalitarian society that removes all oppression and exploitation. That is why he ends the play with: ONE sees Bhoma rising and taking up his rusty axe. His grip becomes stronger. He is grinding his axe, sharpening it. His torn eye lights up with the fire that killed the tiger. While ONE speaks this, everybody gets up slowly, painfully, and blindly. They grope and get at an imaginary axe and try to pick it up. With the last drop of "blood" oozing from his wounds ONE somehow picks up the axe. Then everybody rises in revolt and they start wielding their axes:

> ONE: Strike men—heave ho! Cut down the forests—heave ho!.... Bhoma calls—heave ho! ....The poison plants are growing, heave ho! The poison forests are growing, heave ho! Clear the forest—heave ho! Finish them off—heave ho! On the seaside—heave ho! the harvest comes—heave ho! Bhoma's axe—heave—ho! (110-11)

The finale is grand. It strikes a note of optimism in an artistic style. The image of poisonous trees refers to the class of exploiters and oppressors. K. Sumana has justifiably pointed out: "The society full of opportunists and exploiters is presented as a forest of poisonous trees and Bhoma, an aboriginal barbarian as a woodcutter. Bhoma is an archetype of the oppressed and exploited peasant who, at long last, takes up his 'rusty axe', grinds and sharpens it to cut the poisonous trees that grow around him" (Sumana 65). It throws light on Sircar's vision of Egalitarian society which will be there after cutting down the forest of poisonous trees.

The deterministic forces in life determine man's fate. Whether a person becomes an exploiter or an activist or a worker is determined by his socio-cultural environment. "So, unless and until such oppressive and exploitative socio-cultural environment is exterminated, exploiters and oppressors will continue to exist even if they are annihilated physically." (Babu 138)

Bhoma's cutting down poisonous trees shows his protest against this exploitive and oppressive system. I. Sastri views *Bhoma* as a non-autobiographical presentation of a symbolic search for those Bhomas who may ultimately clear the jungle of poisonous trees, that is, who may clear the society of the legally rooted corrupt members of society. He views this play broadly as "a vehicle towards an egalitarian society." (Sastri N.P.; qtd. in Shampa 193)

Works Cited

Babu, Manchi Sarat. *Indian Drama Today: Study in the Theme of Cultural Deformity*. Prestige, 1997.

Bharucha, Rustom. *Rehearsals of Revolution: The Political Theatre of Bengal*. Seagull Books, 1983.

Bhattacharjee, Shampa. *Badal Sircar's Street Plays: A Thematic Study*. An M. Phil Dissertation. Submitted to Kakatiya University, Warangal. Feb. 1994.

Dutta, Ella. Introduction. *Three Plays*, by Badal Sircar, Seagull, 2009.

Luykx, Nicolaas. "A Public Policy Profile on Rural Development in Bengal." *Aspects of Bengali History and Society*, edited by Rachel Van M. Baumer, Vikas, 1976.

Sastri, I. "Sircar." *Enact*. Jul.-Aug., 1978/1981, N.P.

Sircar, Badal. Preface. *Three Plays*. Seagull, 2009.

———. *On Theatre*. Seagull, 2009.

Sumana, K. "The Importance of Indian Street Theatre with Special Reference to the Plays of Badal Sircar." *Indian Literature Today*, edited by R.K. Dhawan, Prestige, 1994, Vol. I.

(N.B. All textual quotations are from Sircar, Badal. *Three Plays: Procession, Bohma, Stale News*. Seagull, 2009.)

11

Stale News: Spirit for Revolution

Introduction

> What about the courage of man?... What about *Spartacus*, on whose struggles we made a play in 1972? What about all those who dream of and die for the emergence of a new and better society? (Sircar, "Letter" 53)

Badal Sircar was asked these questions by a member of the theatre group "Satabdi", when he was conducting a workshop. After the production of *Gondi*, the "Satabdi" group had no play at hand. They were holding workshops on various burning issues such as: the cruel absurdities we live in, enormous wealth and immeasurable poverty; a flood running hundreds of thousands in the villages, and a huge crowd of fans gathering to see the film stars, construction of the underground railway in Calcutta and ninety percent of the underground water remaining untapped, rendering most of the arable land mono-crop, satellites in space and seventy percent of the population under the poverty line, democracy and police brutality, the absurdity of man, the callousness of man—not just in this country, but in the whole world.

The collage of 'man' in his different aspects formed the subject of a particular workshop. The members collected news clippings and notes of their reactions relating to these aspects of man's callousness, lovelessness, stupidity, and so on. On the basis of these bits of material, discussions were held and it was then that somebody put the above-mentioned questions to the group leader Sircar. The idea emerged amongst the members that the collage did not express the fact that man could protest, man could revolt. So, the theme of the Santhal revolt of 1855-56—that shook the British imperial hold on Eastern India for nine long months—was worked on. Then came further research. (Dutta 8)

The play is based on the revolt of the Santhal tribe which is one of the oldest and largest communities of India on the Bihar-Bengal border. They were tortured not just by the British colonizers but by their own fellow countrymen such as traders, native princes, landlords, etc. "The hungry, the half naked Santhals took up their primitive arms, spear, axe, bow and arrow and fought against the trained, well-fed troops with guns, cannons, horses and elephants, liberating village after village in Bihar and Bengal, not giving up until twenty-five thousand were killed after nine long months of heroic struggle." (Bhattacharjee 204)

Although the play is based on the event that took place long back in history, it goes beyond time and place. Sircar and the other members of the "Satabdi" group decide not to make just a theatrical presentation of this rebellion. Through their research, they became more and more confirmed in the belief that conditions have not changed fundamentally even today. It crosses the boundaries of temporality and eternity and belongs to all times and climes. To put it in Sircar's words:

> But should we make a play on the Santhal revolt of 1855-56,...? The answer was—No. ....We shall show it from our point of view, because we want to link that revolt to the present day reality.... (Sircar, *On* 127)

All the members of "Satabdi" group called material from newspapers, magazines, survey reports—accounts of poverty, exploitation, injustice and atrocities committed against the poorer communities and the repressive measures taken against those who have raised the voice of protest to bring about a change. It is also decided that the play will be performed without characters and dialogues "for they could be false, unconvincing and inadequate" (Sircar, "Letter" 54). The question arises then whose point of view should the play present? Pat comes Sircar's reply: "We decided to show it from the point of view of a contemporary young man just like any of us..." (Sircar, "Letter" 54). He is a middle-class, urban man. He is educated. He appears rather disturbed, since he is constantly bombarded by lots of information from textbooks, newspapers, radio, and literature—false, true, even irrelevant. Sometimes he comes across a report of mass killing or gang-rape in an aboriginal village by the paid gangsters of the local upper caste landlords. Sometimes, it may be a survey report giving facts and figures regarding bonded labour for a whole lifetime, sometimes for generations. "He is confused by this bombardment of a barrage of information, quite often contradictory, full of contrasts and perhaps even the most shattering bits of information come as stale news" (Dutta 8). Similarly, the man is attending his daily routines such as going through the exams, entertaining himself with movies, wandering in the search of a job. Sircar further informs:

> If that young man also happens to read an account of the Santhal revolt, what happens? Will his defence mechanism succeed in making him forget all that thereby allowing him to concentrate on his career, his personal life, his family affairs? Or will he change a little, will he make a decision, make a choice, however minor, to do something about it? (Sircar, "Letter" 55)

This thinking encouraged the group to evolve the play, *Stale News*. So, it is observed that the members of "Satabdi" made a great contribution through writing and production of this play. It was collectively researched and shaped by the whole group. Sircar wrote the text of the play only after it was fully investigated by the group.

The Structure of the Play

One of the main purposes of *Stale News* is to show "how the Santhals revolted". Sircar is interested in man's courage in fighting injustice. He knows "how the colonial interests of a foreign nation sucked the blood of a vast rural land which perhaps is the true India". Hence, identifying the British rule or colonialism as the prime cause of rebellion appears to be his motive in writing the play. (Bhattacharjee 246)

Sircar is greatly influenced by the Santhal revolt, since he feels that this revolt has indicated a way to the Indian people. "...thanks to the great rebellion which developed into the broad highway of India's struggle for freedom. That highway extends into the twentieth century..." (Ray 34; qtd. in Ranjit 31-32). While criticizing colonialism, Sircar also aims to expose the Bengali middle-class during the British Raj that performed the collaborationist role. British people cunningly created this class to strengthen their grip on the ruled. They acted as 'the lackeys of the British' (135) and served the colonialist at the war front. Sircar is worried to find that this middle-class continues to promote the cultural legacy of the colonialist even during this post-colonial period. The play exposes the fact that conditions have not changed fundamentally even today. Therefore, the subject of the Santhal rebellion is contemporary.

In the course of action, 'The Dead Man' wanders amongst the chorus of performers. He holds his bandaged left palm in front of the eyes of a performer to make him read something about the Santhals of the last century and right palm for something happening today. The pairs of performers wait for their turn to rise and go round with their statements, and kneel down once they deliver their accounts of facts, views and problems.

It has been presented in the play that the Santhals cleared the inaccessible forests, "raised a golden harvest on a land that had never been trod upon by human feet" (125). They sent large quantities of rice and oil to the cities and received, in return, a small sum of earth, some salt, tobacco or cloth. "At the slightest sign of protest, donkeys, horses, cattle and even elephants were let loose on their fields to destroy their crops and teach them a lesson" (132). The peaceful, poor, illiterate Santhals were cheated and forced out of their property; their vegetables, goats and poultry were snatched away; insults, beatings, torture, the rape of their women—nothing was left out. To get a loan, they had to sign a bond of perpetual slavery and "the British rulers were concerned only with collecting revenue." (133)

It took the moneylenders, landlords and British rulers a long time to realize that the movement never remained confined to the Santhals only. It inspired the other downtrodden such as the blacksmiths, the potters, the milkmen, the oil pressers, the leather-workers, the sweepers, all the other 'low caste' Hindus and the poor Muslim weavers in Birbhum, Murshidabad, Bhagalpur, etc.

Later on, the play depicts the movement of the so-called Bengal Renaissance or Re-awakening. "Zamindars. Mutsuddis. Traders. Professors. Teachers. Clerks. Caste Hindus. The lackeys of the British. Contractors" (135) participated in the 'movement' to emphasize that "without the support of the English, there is no way to revive the eternal religion" (138) and that "The English are friendly Rulers." (138)

The Renaissance did not alter the lives of the poor masses even a little. From the revolt emerged the legendary leaders of the Santhal Hool. They swore to throw out all exploiters and oppressors from the "Santhal country" and to reclaim all their land. They swore to establish an independent Santhal state. That set the tone of the battle and they declared that the *hool* was on (July 7, 1855) (148). *Hool* for the Santhals is 'revolt'.

The Santhals then killed the police personnel, looted the houses of moneylenders after killing them, plundered the palaces of the zamindars, and raided the English indigo outposts. A few thousand soldiers were brought in to help the police in crushing the revolt. There was a fierce battle on July 16 for five hours. But they could not defeat the Santhals. The commissioner of Bhagalpur, in distress, asked the Lieutenant-Governor Lord Dalhousie to declare martial law immediately and announced rewards for the arrest of the leaders of the *hool*.

The entire military force of the eastern region was concentrated at one point to check the progress of the revolt. Zamindars and moneylenders provided weapons, arranged for food and shelter and night halts for the army on the march. The indigo planters provided men and money in plenty. The Nawab of Murshidabad sent fifty elephants also to crush the Santhals, their wives and children under their feet and to raze their huts.

In the final battle, thirty to fifty thousand half-naked rebels with their primitive weapons prepare to face fifteen thousand trained soldiers armed with guns and cannons. Nearly twenty-five Santhals were killed and all their leaders died one by one. "They died, but were not defeated. Not a single Santhal rebel surrendered" (155). "The idea of surrender was alien to the Santhals" (156). As long as the revolt raged, the British, all over India, lived in panic.

Santhal revolt took place long back in 1856. But the situation has not changed yet in the 20th century. It is portrayed in the play that the place of Santhals is taken by the tribals, Harijans and the other downtrodden people. Even today thousands of tribals, Harijans and so many others die of starvation. Seventy percent population live below the poverty line "attractive jingles-advertising costly cosmetics and luxury goods and gadgets are broadcast on radio and TV and Blow Hot plays and films of love run for hundreds of nights". Ninety percent of the people live below the basic nutrition line and thousands of low caste people are forced to sign the bonds enslaving themselves for life and forced to stay as bonded labour, while "hundreds of crores of rupees are spent on renovation of palaces, while funds are not available for preventing the devastating floods." (Bhattacharjee 256)

In the remaining section of the play, the events in the nineteenth and the twentieth centuries are depicted simultaneously. These events of the massacre are a burning example of the fact that India as pointed out by V.S. Naipaul is..."*A Million Mutinies, Now*" (Naipaul, *Million*) for ever. The inhuman treatment given to the Santhals in the 19th century and to the Harijans and other low caste people in the 20th century brings to notice the naked reality that our country is still..."*A Wounded Civilization.*" (Naipaul, *Wounded*)

While describing the reality in the 20th century, Sircar writes:

> One hundred and fifty workers were killed, figures for the injured are not available. The dead bodies were later piled up in a sugarcane field and set on fire (160).... In August 1971, more than 150 people were killed in two days.... The dead bodies lay on the street in the

> clear daylight before they were lifted up in rickshaws and handcarts and deposited in the Hooghly river. A 60-year-old man was soaked in petrol and burnt to death because he could not give the killers any information about his nephew. (161)

Women are doubly victimized: at their homes and in the offices. The women of the downtrodden workers are distorted, insulted, and raped. While depicting the predicament of women in society, Sircar writes: "A woman cannot stand and wait all by herself at a bus-stop" (130). "Offices are closed on Sundays, half days on Saturdays." But women "have to work every day. No festivals, no special days" (122). They are also ill-treated by their in-laws.

Observing the repetition of Santhal revolt, that is, history in the post independence society, Sircar comes to the conclusion that:

> Death, blood and fear rule over this land. Everyone knows what happens and what will happen behind the prison walls. (163)

Either rise in revolt or find yourself behind the bars—that is the clear message of the plays for the millions and millions of the downtrodden in the country.

Critical Interpretation and Appraisal of the Play

The play *Stale News* is based on the Santhal Revolt that took place in 1855-56. But it is not a historical play. Using the episode from history, Sircar conveys that social inequality, exploitation, oppression, suppression are the characteristics of all societies in all ages. He states:

> At a certain point in my life, I happen to come across the history of the Santhal revolt and that disturbing element within me gets strengthened, threatening to affect my so-called 'sane' choices. That is the way we should link the Santhal revolt of the last century to our present day experiences, through the experience of a protagonist of our kind. (Sircar, *On* 127)

The play *Stale News* has been made by the group collectively. Sircar says: "At a later stage, I made a script on the basis of the materials collected and the decisions made. Whatever I contributed, I did during the process like any other member, and not when I made the script. As such, I am not the author of the play, at best the editor. Making a script in this way is a unique feature in the history of our group, and also what makes it a unique voyage." (Sircar, *On* 129)

In *Stale News*, Sircar examines and analyses the exploitation and oppression of the Santhals of the British/Colonial India and that of the Harijans and other downtrodden people of the post-colonial India. The statement "Man is the greatest creature" is used as a refrain to throw light on the meaninglessness and absurdity of his achievements. That human beings were not treated as humans in the past and will not be treated so in the present and in the future seems to be the message of the play.

Sircar juxtaposes the events of the past and the present through the technique of a Dead Man. The Dead Man is the symbol of dead humanity. His whole body is dressed in white and his head and face, including his eyes are covered with bandages. He does not utter a single word in the play. He enters and exits as per the necessity of the situation. The fact that he has been killed is symbolically suggested right at the beginning of the play. Sircar says: "The killed man was to be the visual representation of the disturbing element in the mind of the protagonist, thus he would be generally invisible to all except him, or the others would treat him as an ordinary person" (Sircar, *On* 128). The dead man holds his palm in front of the eyes of the protagonist at reading distance and the protagonist read out like a hypnotized person. The dead man shows his left palm for the past and his right palm for the present, that is, for contemporary newspaper items. "And towards the end of the play, the dead man would go on holding his palms alternately when the two periods would be finally linked up." (Sircar, *On* 128)

At the beginning of the play, the actors mime the birth of ONE and then his education from school to college. As a grown-up man, ONE is delineated as bombarded with various news items and statements relating to his surrounding environment. At the same time, he learns about the Santhals and their revolt. He appears too confused to take any decision. However, he, somehow, continues his routine life, i.e. completes his education, gets a job and marries a woman. This shows man's indifference and lovelessness towards his fellowmen.

The Santhal revolt that took place in the nineteenth century was ruthlessly crushed by the British colonizers with the help of some Indian landlords, moneylenders in pre-independence days. But the situation has not changed in the post-colonial period. The post-independence Indian Government has proved itself as bad as the British Government. So, the ugly, abominable deformity of the Indian society remains the same. It is observed that the Indian Government has done little to improve the conditions of the poor and the downtrodden and always remained in favour of the rich. Ultimately, victim-victimizer relationship becomes a permanent feature of our society, pre-independent as well as post-independent.

The ruthless exploitation and massacre of the Santhals by the British and that of the downtrodden by the Indian authorities bring to notice that our country has been *The Waste Land* which is characterized with spiritual sterility. The death of the man symbolizes the death of humanity in the so-called cultured, civilized contemporary society.

> Where the world has not been broken up into fragments by narrow domestic walls....
>
> Into that heaven of freedom, my father, let my country awake. (Tagore 33)

says Rabindranath Tagore in one of his songs from the *Gitanjali*. However, the ideal is not transformed into the real. Instead, what W.B. Yeats says in his revolutionary, epoch-making poem "The Second Coming":

> The best lack all conventions, while the worst
> Are full of passionate intensity. (Yeats 253)

becomes the universal truth. The incidents, that manifest hatred between man and man result in merciless violence, are the normal events or incidents in the Indian society.

Massacre and bloodshed, violence and exploitation become the permanent characteristics of Indian society since people fail to understand what "freedom" is in the true sense of that word. Pondering over the dark, horrifying condition of the Indian society, one feels that things have gone awry and vested interests create hurdles in the establishment of a casteless and classless society. Actually, what happened in India is:

> ...the rabble with their well-worn creeds,
> Their large professions and their little deeds,
> Mingle in selfish strife, lo, freedom weeps,
> Wrong rules the land, and waiting justice sleeps.

as said in the school textbook. (Holand 174)

Manchi Sarat Babu points out: "The...tribal people living on the mountains in Srikakulam of Andhra Pradesh, revolted against the exploitation and oppression of landlords, moneylenders and government officials in 1969, more than one century after the Santhal Revolt. It was also mercilessly suppressed. Thus, the play will continue to be relevant as long as the social deformity, in conjunction with other deformities, lasts." (Babu 55)

Sircar has criticized not only the ruling class but the middle class also that remains supportive to this exploitation, although indirectly. For Veena Noble Dass, "The play attempted to expose the collaborationist role of the Bengali middle class during the British Raj (Das 78). It is for this reason that Sircar chooses his protagonist from the middle class people. To quote Ella Dutta again: "What is important is that he is confused by the bombardment of a barrage of information, quite often contradictory, full of contrasts and perhaps even the most shattering bits of information come as stale news." (Dutta 8)

Towards the end of the play, Sircar explores the fact in the contemporary society. About the Santhal revolt, the protagonist's remark is: "But all this happened so long ago.... This is the twentieth century" (159). It is observed that in the contemporary society, people are in rat-race. They stoop so low to achieve their target in the shortest possible time that they do not hesitate a least to kick their companions, even seniors out of the race. In every field, "the lackeys of the British" appear as the agents of the new regime which proved itself to be "the same old staff with a new flag".

In the context of the cultural decadence, degradation and nihilism, that rule over the whole country, how should a healthy-minded citizen react? Sircar wishes to discuss this with someone, who can spare some time. He is in the search of a man, who is not scared of anybody. He wants to see whether "a middle-class young man changes a little when he happens to read an account of the Santhal revolt?" (Sircar, "Letter" 55) The playwright wishes to put the young man through the acid test to find whether his defence mechanism succeeds in making him forget all about his career, his personal life, his family affairs to take a decision for doing something, however minor, for the cause for which twenty-five thousand Santhals shed their blood that was "washed into the drains, from the drains into the rivers, from the rivers into the sea. Scientists will no doubt manufacture something useful from this blood-saturated sea water one day, for something as valuable as blood should not be split in vain" (159). So voices the playwright in the garb of a performer.

The throbs of the anguished heart of the writer give life to this play. For him, the Santhal revolt of 1855 is not at all "Stale News". In fact, it is stop-press item for him (Bhattacharjee 260). Here, Sircar and his group attempt to awake the people: to make them cherish the memory of all those who dream of and die for the emergence of a new and better society, where people have "visions and revisions". The play is full of violence, massacre and sensationalism. But it ends on an optimistic note because, the young man, who remains indifferent to the sensational items in a newspaper since he wanted to lead a normal routine life is delineated as or transformed into a rebel who revolts against the capitalist society. The play ends with him calling upon the people to react by raising their voice against the system:

> Death, blood and fear rule over this land. Everyone knows what happens and what will happen behind the prison walls. Why don't you scream? Is it still not time? Not time? (Other actors join him. The voices rise to a crescendo). (163-64)

Works Cited

Babu, Manchi Sarat. *Indian Drama Today: Study in the Theme of Cultural Deformity*. Prestige, 1997.

Bhattacharjee, Shampa. *Badal Sircar's Street Plays: A Thematic Study*. An M. Phil. Dissertation submitted to Kakátiya University, Warangal, 1994.

Das, Veena Noble. *Modern Indian Drama in English Translation*. 1988.

Dutta, Ella. Introduction. *Three Plays*, by Badal Sircar. Seagull, 2009.

Holand, J.G. "True Men." *English Reader: Kumar Bharati*. Std. IX. Maharashtra State Board of Secondary Education, 1994.

Naipaul, V.S. Blurb. *India: A Million Mutinies, Now*. Penguin, 1995.

———. Blurb. *India: A Wounded Civilization*. Penguin, 1979.

Ray, Suprakash, and Bharater Krishak Bidroha O Ganatantrik Sangam. Vol. I, 1996, quoted by Ranjit Guha. "The Prose of Counter Insurgency." *Subaltern Studies-II. Writings on South Asian History and Society.* OUP, 1993.

Sircar, Badal. "A Letter from Badal Sircar." *The Drama Review* (US). Vol. 26, No. 2, Summer, 1982.

———. *On Theatre*. Seagull, 2009.

Tagore, Rabindranath. "Where the Mind is without Fear." *Gitanjali*. Macmillan, 2004.

Yeats, W.B. "The Second Coming." *Six English Poets*, edited by V. Sachitanadan. Macmillan, 1978.

(N.B. All textual quotations are from Sircar, Badal. *Three Plays*. Seagull, 2009.)

12

Indian History Made Easy: India—Yesterday and Today

Introduction

The post-independence period witnessed the rise of the cultural movements like the Progressive Writers' Association (PWA) in 1936 and the Indian People's Theatre Association (IPTA) in 1943. "The IPTA's purpose was clear-cut from the beginning: to portray, through the medium of the stage and other traditional arts, details of external aggression by the fascist, internal repression by a colonial government, and the disintegration of the economic life with an intention to enlighten the Indians about their possible role in solving these problems." (Pradhan 151; qtd. in Sarkar xi-xii)

People joined hands against the emerging trends of capitalism, imperialism and fascism and provided a strong support to the Communist Party of India, worker's associations and peasant movements. The 'Gana Natya Andolon' (People's Theatre Movement) and the 'Naba Natya' (New Theatre) indicated a total break with the traditional Bengali theatre. It had initiated the beginning of the New Drama Movement in Bengal during the 40s and the 50s.

The pioneering playwrights in Bengal like Sambhu Mitra, Utpal Dutt, Ajitesh Bandyopadhyay, and Badal Sircar started using the stage to explore the socio-psychological spectrum of the predicament of modern man in a country that was going through its cultural and ideological revisionary phase in the post-colonial era.

Badal Sircar (1925-2011) was one of the most important playwrights in the contemporary Indian theatre, who made significant contribution not only in the content but also in the form to make theatre the people's theatre in the post-independent phase of Indian drama. His 'Third Theatre' is a departure from the urban, proscenium theatre and rural, folk theatre which aims at giving the audience-oriented, open-air, non-proscenium performances. According to Aparna Dharwadker, "During the 1960s, Sircar became interested in developing minimalist theatre that could provide an alternative to urban realist drama as well as rural folk forms and attract audiences in both locations. His conception of this 'Third Theatre' in India was strongly mediated by Jerzy Grotowski's 'Poor Theatre' and Richard Schechner's 'Environmental Theatre', both of which he encountered while travelling in Europe and North America on a Nehru Fellowship. Since the early 1970s, these avant-garde influences have led Sircar to develop largely, body-centred vehicles for non-proscenium indoor performance, outdoor urban environments, such as large parks and open grounds, and extensive tours in rural areas. His theatre is intimate, emotionally intense, detached from political dogma, opposed to the commodification of art, and committed to communication—between the performers and the spectators as well as within the members of each group." (Dharwadker 65-66)

Sircar started his career as a playwright, actor and director in the early 1950s with the proscenium stage as a medium of communication. By the late fifties, he came out with six comedies: *Solution X* (1956), *Baropisima* ('The Elder Aunt', 1959), *Shanibar* ('Saturday', 1959), *Ram, Shyam, Jadu* ('Tom, Dick, Harry', 1961), *Ballabhpurer Rupkatha* ('The Fairy Tale of Ballabhpur', 1963), and *Kabikahani* ('A Tale of a Poet', 1964). The second phase of Sircar's career constituted his experimental quest. During this phase, he started exploring serious issues about contemporary Indian society. His major proscenium plays in this phase include *Baki Itihas* ('That Other History', 1965), *Tringsha Shatabdi* ('The Thirtieth Century', 1966), and *Pagla Ghoda* ('Mad Horse', 1967). However, it was with the publication of *Ebong Indrajit* ('Evam Indrajit', 1963) he got the recognition as one of the leading playwrights of the Indian theatre.

During the 70s, Sircar employed the theorisation of the 'Third Theatre' for the performances of his plays such as *Procession* (Michhil, 1972), *Scandal in Fairyland* (Rupkathar Kelenkari, 1975), *Indian History Made Easy* (Sukhapathya Bharater Itihas, 1976), *Beyond the Land of Hattamala* (Hatamalar Opare, 1977), *Stale News* (Bashi Khobor, 1978), *Bhoma* (1979), etc.

While commenting on the structure of the play Sircar writes, "Communication is essential in every art form; the artist communicates to other people through literature, music, painting, and acting. But the methods of communication are different. A writer writes—he does not have to be present when his writing is being read.... In cinema, the film artists do not have to be present when the film is being projected. But in theatre, the performers have to be present when the communication takes place. This is a fundamental difference. Theatre is a live show, cinema is not. In theatre, communication is direct; in cinema it is through images." (Sircar 11)

The Structure of the Play

Indian History Made Easy deals with the theme of British colonialism, the most significant period in the history of India. It starts from the establishment of the East-India Company and ends at the point of Indian independence and partition in 1947. Classroom is used as the platform for the performance of the play, where teachers, students, the master and two women characters namely, Britannia and Mother India constitute the different roles in the process of making the entire period come alive. The play covers more than three hundred years of the British rule without the coherent structure of plot as is the usual practice of Sircar. According to Subhendu Sarkar, "...though the students are taught, it is actually the audience who learns about the mechanism of colonial exploitation. In this respect, *Sukhapathya Bharater Itihas* bears close resemblance to Brecht's *Lehrstucke* (Learning play)." (Sarkar xxxi)

As the class starts, a woman carrying a Union Jack walks in a slow, relaxed manner on a platform at the end of the hall. The jubilant cheer by the teachers: "Three cheers for Robert Clive!... Three cheers for the battle of Plassey!... Three Cheers for the East India Company! Hip hip hurray!" (11) reveal their colonial affinity and their subservience to a dead past. The woman with the Union Jack is addressed as, 'Mom, Mom Britannia' (13). The teachers enact the role of a dutiful son before their mother. They inform her about all the money that has been accumulated by the East India Company.

BRITANNIA: You had dewani of *East India* for six years. How much did you send me, son? (13)

TEACHERS (sing): Everything we'll surrender to your feet. Everything we'll surrender to your feet. (14)

The conversation between Britannia and the teachers reveals the exploitative nature of the colonial rule in India. Meanwhile, Britannia ceases to be a mother figure and acquires the position of a Goddess. In response to her transformation, the teachers and the students form a make-believe palanquin by making use of a few props like umbrella and move around the room singing, 'Everything we'll surrender to your feet' (14). It is observed that "Some hold an 'umbrella', some a 'flywhisk', some a 'fan'. Some play the tune 'God save the King' (14) by blowing imaginary trumpets. Mother Britannia enjoys the celebration and responds to their obedience quite graciously saying: "Now my precious son's bringing gold and silver from India. My banks are swelling, investing money. What's the worry about factories now? ...my lulululululu!" (16)

With the exit of Mother Britannia, the playwright focuses on the history lesson, while the students get restless in class. With the introduction of a new term in their lesson—'Industrial Revolution'—the class breaks up and the teachers and the students form themselves into a machine. It works making a wild sound. While their legs and hands move rhythmically with pistons, a destitute woman rushes into the stage with a prolonged scream. The teachers continue saying 'More, More' in a low tone. Their bodies suggest exploitation and plunder and their eyes greed. Through their action, Sircar provides the audience with a commentary on the nature of the economic exploitation carried out by the British.

In the play, the destitute woman in her spoiled clothes and dishevelled hair represents MA that is 'Mother India'. Her untidy appearance embodies the predicament of our country under the British Raj. She is an exact antithesis to the portrayal of Britannia. Ironically, the three teachers strolled around the room like petty British officers, chanting: "We want more! Want more! Want more!" (19)

The three teachers turn into vultures. They speak at the nearly-dead bodies of the students and MA. Their gestures signify the ugly, heavy creatures that move from one corpse to another. Eventually, Sircar shifts the attention of the audience to the reign of Lord Cornwallis—the Governor General of India, as the audience are informed that the "*Mercantile Capital is replaced by Industrial Capital*" (22) in India.

However, the chaotic Indian history makes the class more disorganized and riotous. The First World War and the Quit India Movement bring about a change in the mind-set of the Indian people. Even the teachers abandon their former roles as the sycophants of the British. Ironically, they are transformed into the emerging national leaders of India. But the master continues to support the British Raj, and the teachers demand for capitalist wealth and material satisfaction.

The students and the teachers march around the room chanting slogans against the supremacy of the British Raj. But the master grabs the destitute woman and violently throws her on the floor. He leaves the room declaring, "The class is over! History is over! Over!" (46) The members of the chorus re-enter the stage to participate energetically in a freedom chant. However, mother India informs the audience the anticipated situation in the post-independence India which consists of more deaths. Gradually, the freedom chant loses its intensity. It merges into cries of despair, pleas for food and intense lamentation. Significantly, Sircar juxtaposes the celebration of India's independence with the images of the world of destitution and famine. (Mukherjee; qtd. in the criterion 231)

The British colonizers quit India by giving the gift of divided Hindustan and the spirit of colonialism once and forever. The country was divided into India and Pakistan. The ending of the play is "an insidious reminder of the emergence of the bourgeois class and the omnipresence of the capitalist culture in the post-independent phase of India." (Mukherjee; qtd. in the criterion 231)

Critical Interpretation and Appraisal of the Play

The play opens and ends on the same note. It seems to provide a comment on the unchanged miserable condition of the Indian peasants and the agricultural labourers after centuries of rule by various kings and governments and even in the post-independence period. The performance takes the form of a history class with teachers and students. Subhendu Sarkar opines: "*Sukhapathya Bharater Itihas* (*Indian History Made Easy*) lays bare one of the most crucial periods in the history of India—British colonialism. What is even more significant about the play is the relation between form and content. To match the content, Sircar uses the form of classroom teaching. Therefore, with the Teachers instructing the Students, he could easily cover more than three hundred years of British rule without developing a 'Story'. (Sarkar xxxi)

The performance of the play in the classroom explores the Indian history through the three main periods of colonial rule till independence. England is portrayed as Mother Britannia who first sends her loved son, the East India Company to plunder India and establish Merchant Capital. The teaching of history signifies how this plunder forms the basis of the Industrial Revolution in Britain. It is observed that the village society is crushed each time. A new ruler fights for more profit. Each time society tries to rebuild itself, but remains as submerged in bitter poverty and servitude as before. Sircar seems to convey that exploitation, oppression, suppression, subjugation are the characteristic features of all societies in all times.

Along with the theme of east-west encounter, Sircar here seems to explore into the pros and cons of the educational system in India. The repetition of words and the modes of interrogation and response: 'Good...Very Good...Clear?...Yes sir' (4-5) throws light on the futility of the teaching process while the prayer-song skilfully mocks at the ineffective academic scenario in contemporary India, where education intends to impart mere information in the name of knowledge. The educational system in India provides a little scope to the students' participation in the process. What actually happens in the classroom is a monologue, not very dramatic. The teacher goes on explaining and the students sit as the passive listeners. Their doubts cannot be solved. They are not given the opportunity to ask questions during the class. It is indicated in the play that they repeat all the words of their teachers with an appalling subservience. The repetition of the words used by the teachers: 'Rama... Shyam... Raj... Rajo... Ramrajo... Shyamrajo... Gramshomaj' (4-5) reinforces the ridiculous thought process of the teachers. While criticising the classroom teaching in the city of Calcutta, Rustom Bharucha justifiably states: "With a hundred thousand students in Calcutta University, it is a widely accepted fact that most students view a university education as the only alternative to unemployment. Apart from this frustration and the fact that results may not be published for six to eight months after an examination (among other administrative problems), the structure, teaching methods and curriculum of Calcutta University remain intrinsically colonial. This is the most disheartening aspect of education in Calcutta: its adherence to models prescribed by the British." (Bharucha 169-70)

The money looted from India turns into Britain's initial capital. Commodities are provided at the cost of Indian market. "Juxtaposing the academic axiom spouted by the teachers, Sircar informs the audience that the British are suppressing the growth of the industries in India by forcing the natives to buy goods manufactured in Britain. The extent of the commercial exploitation has been exemplified by the playwright in the conversation between Britannia and the master which reveals the tragic scenario of the Indian industry during the colonial period." (Mukherjee; qtd. in the criterion 227)

MASTER: You've ruined my business to provide him with the Market, mom....

BRITANNIA: ...you take pride in selling goods made by others! Get lost! Now goods from my lululu's factories will hit India. (23-24)

While commenting on the exploitation of India by the British, Sircar says: "In the first phase of colonial exploitation, the products of the highly developed cottage industries of India were purchased at unfair rates by the East India Company...and cities like Calcutta, Bombay, Madras were created to serve as centres for collecting and exporting such products to Europe. The capital accumulated through such exploitation enabled Britain to complete her Industrial Revolution" (Sircar 87). Naturally, the Indian cottage industries that tended to compete with the British industries were systematically destroyed. The British were doubly benefited as India was converted into a backward agricultural country to serve as a gigantic market for British industrial goods on the one hand, and to supply raw material to the British industries on the other. It is noticed in the play that the establishment of the zamindari system proved to be a very effective means for the colonizers to achieve these ends. So, it was cunningly strengthened and consolidated by them.

The ultimate impact of industrial revolution in England was that there was a growing demand for foreign goods in India and a subsequent impoverishment among the Indian. The song sung by the teachers and the students in the praise of Britannia "If it's Permanent Settlement,/ The British sun will never set" (29) shows the sincerity and devotion of the Indians to the colonial rule. Their own mother's scream on the death of her sons affected them in the least. Sircar has juxtaposed the image of two mothers in this scene. Britannia is being worshipped by the Indians in expectation of capitalist gain and material comfort and they turned deaf ear to their mother's cry and remained blind to her plight.

Throughout the play, one can easily feel the constant ethos of colonial dominance in India. The most discordant reminders occur when the teachers demonstrate their use of English language: "Yes, sir, No, sir. Very good, sir. Good morning, sir. Good evening, sir. I remain, sir, your obedient servant..." (30). According to Rustom Bharucha these words epitomize the 'fundamental subservience of babu English' which is the most pervasive legacy of the British rule in India. (Bharucha 162)

The skilful performance of the play in the classroom creates a live picture of the forced development of industry in India, the laying of railways for the efficient distribution of goods and supply of raw material, the agony of the villagers and the contradictions in the exploitative system. The enactment is played in a series of climaxes, as each period ends and the peasantry and working class is back where it ever was. It is communicated through the demand of the students: "Give us food. Give us food" (50). The height of the irony lies in the joining of the Master with Britannia in the Ballroom dancing, who covers herself in a cloth with a 'Dollar' sign. The play ends with a note that the bourgeois class in India enters into a new alliance, this time with the "Mother Dollar". To quote it, in the words of Vijay Tendulkar, the play ends with the note: "The show must go on." (Tendulkar 120)

Works Cited

Bharucha, Rustom. *Rehearsals of Revolution: The Political Theatre of Bengal.* Seagull Books, 1982.

Dharwadker, Aparna Bhargava. *Theatres of Independence: Drama, Theory and Urban Performance in India Since 1947.* Oxford University Press, 2005.

Mukherjee, Victor. "Exploring the Aesthetics of the 'Third Theatre': A Study of Badal Sircar's *Indian History Made Easy", quoted in* www.the-criterion.com *The Criterion: An International Journal in English.* Vol. 7, Issue I, February 2016.

Pradhan, Sudhi, editor. *Marxist Cultural Movement in India: Chronicles and Documents* (1936-1947), Vol. I. Santi Pradhan, 1985.

Sarkar, Subhendu. Introduction. *Two Plays: Indian History Made Easy, Life of Bagala*, by Badal Sircar, OUP, 2010.

Sircar, Badal. *On Theatre.* Seagull Books, 2009.

Tendulkar, Vijay. *Silence! The Court is in Session*, (53-121), occurred in *Collected Plays in Translation.* OUP, 2003.

(N.B. All textual quotations are from Sircar, Badal. *Two Plays: Indian History Made Easy, Life of Bagala.* OUP, 2010.)

The Last Phase: Fairy-tale-based Non-proscenium Plays

13

Life of Bagala: Where there is Will, there is Way

Introduction

Badal Sircar is recognized as one of the innovators of the contemporary Indian theatre with his contribution of nearly fifty plays, some of which are translated into major Indian languages. Though a trained civil engineer and town planner, he took a keen interest in the theatre of the day. Disappointed by the contemporary conventional Bengali theatre, he began writing plays from the 1950s. His early plays include comedies about everyday life of the middle-class people of Calcutta. In his later plays, he is concerned with the pointlessness of man's existence, lovelessness and callousness of man towards man, his indifference to responsibilities, his sense of guilt in a world of increasing violence and inhumanity.

With his idea of Anganmanch or the Third Theatre, he abandoned proscenium stage and performed plays in a bare room or in an open space with spectators sitting all around. Thus, his theatre successfully broke the barriers between a performer and spectators and created an easy communication between the actors and the audience. He wanted the theatre to be a collective exercise to awaken and enhance the social consciousness of people. In the process, he achieved the involvement of villagers with whom he lived during the process of some plays in writing and production.

The Third Theatre is flexible, portable and inexpensive, since Sircar here totally avoided the use of props, costumes and other equipments. Naturally, the firm grip of the constituent parts of drama, that is, theme, characterization, etc., gets loose here. In his plays, there is a direct address to the audience, which makes them introspective. And therein lays the success of his plays.

The play *Life of Bagala* (*Bagalacharitmanas* 1998) does not deal with the serious issues found in other plays of Sircar. Instead, it tells a story of a simple, straightforward man named Bagalacharan Batabyal. The playwright successfully tries to make it interesting and full of humour by using the technique of a magical lighter like that of Aladdin's lamp. However, the outwardly comic play gives a rational message towards its end. It is the only play, where the pure humour of the early period and the serious message of the Third Theatre phase are combined. (Sarkar xxix)

The Outline of Story in Brief

The play opens with two Stage Managers standing together to blow their imaginary trumpets on the arrival of the hero. They repeat the imaginary action but no hero enters. They search for the hero in the audience. Suddenly a simple, ordinary person named Bagalacharan Batabyal comes out from the crowd, showing his frustration and disillusionment towards life, saying: "Rather than hanging this name round its neck they should've tied a 10 kg stone and thrown the child into the Ganges!" (54) Bagala, having lost his parents in childhood, is brought up and educated by his uncle and aunt. Even after performing the household chores and tutoring his nephew sincerely, he receives nothing but constant humiliation.

The play depicts the childhood and college days of Bagala, when he used to be made a laughing-stock by all those surrounding him. In addition to his untidy appearance, his grotesque name (Bagalacharan Batabyal) provides a chance to others to tease him. The continuous insult and humiliation render him introvert. The graduation degree does not raise his level of confidence, which ultimately leads to the unsuccessful performance in the interview.

His aunt's and uncle's decision of his marriage with an ugly, quarrelsome and pampered girl of a wealthy man just for the sake of money brings about a change in the mind-set of Bagala. He leaves the house and tries to commit suicide by putting his head on the railway track. However, he is miraculously saved by the Nilapari, a genie who has the magical power and works wonders for her master, the Old Man.

The sympathetic treatment meted out to Bagala by the Old Man and Nilapari helps him to regain his confidence. They successfully encourage Bagala to be bold enough to defy his uncle and aunt. With their encouragement, he returns to his uncle's house and faces the situation quite bravely. Throwing the money bag at the uncle, he left them once and forever. The play ends with the Old Man leaving for a pilgrimage quite satisfactorily and Bagala getting a job and teaching Nila how to do the household chores.

Critical Interpretation and Appraisal of the Play

The play *Life of Bagala* presents a humorous story with an oblique political import (Sircar, Blurb). Bagala's life-story brings to notice how constant humiliation reduces one's life to slavery and generosity helps one regain self-confidence. It also illuminates the fact that human will and determination alone can make one stand on his feet instead of living in the world of magic.

The play depicts the transformation in the character of Bagala, from a simple, timid, introvert man into a rational and courageous person. However, not only Bagala but Nila, the genie, also changes 180 degree in the course of the play. (Sarkar xxix)

The protagonist of the play Bagala proves the fact that it is only by acquiring guts that one can lead to self-determination and can live a normal life of peace and satisfaction. "It should be noted that an abusive word (*sala*) plays a significant part in making Bagala bold." (Sarkar xxix)

Outwardly, the play appears comic, but it gives a serious message that, in achieving success, no short-cuts are available. There is always some room on the top. However, it is through a firm determination, strong will and confident action that one can achieve the goal. The concluding lines of the chorus reinforce this message:

> Magic doesn't help a real attempt
> Do away with it at this moment
> Come with brooms, running
> Clean the filth by sweeping...
> Sloth, coward, idler—all
> Brooms, in your hands, have a ball. (110)

To conclude the discussion with the remark of Subhendu Sarkar: "Apart from fantasy, humour is also an effective means of sowing Badal Sircar's ideas. Though he did not write any full-length comedy after the hilarious proscenium plays at the beginning of his career, it does not necessarily imply that humour completely disappeared from Sircar's repertoire" (Sarkar xxix). The play *Life of Bagala* proves this fact and "aptly demonstrates how varied Sircar's plays are." (Sarkar xxx)

Works Cited

Sarkar, Subhendu. Introduction. *Two Plays: Indian History Made Easy, Life of Bagala*, by Badal Sircar, OUP, 2010.

Sircar, Badal. Blurb. *Two Plays: Indian History Made Easy, Life of Bagala*. OUP, 2010.

(N.B. All textual quotations are from Sircar, Badal. *Two Plays: Indian History Made Easy, Life of Bagala*. OUP, 2010.)

14

Scandal in Fairyland: Media—A Fairyland of Never-ending Scandals

Introduction

Badal Sircar is seen as one who gives a new direction and dimension to the Indian drama by his Third Theatre. Majority of his plays deal with the theme of self-evaluation. Sircar firmly believes that development is possible only when people will be critically aware of their situation, their responsibilities, and their potentialities to bring about a change in society.

The play *Scandal in Fairyland,* written in 1974, is an adaptation of a story of Premendra Mitra's "Roopkathar Kelenkari" with some differences. Premendra's work is a story written for children and Sircar's work is a play written for adults. In an interview on the 19th July 1991, he has told Samik Bandyopadhyay that he has never written a play specially for children, because it is so hard to write for children. But at the same time, he admits that whatever is thematically valuable in his play has come from the story of Premendra Mitra. (Bandyopadhyay viii)

In this play, Sircar has made the use of a dream-world in which wealth plays a vital role. However, he connects the dreamy world to the present day reality through the character of a newspaper-boy who, he explains, his improvisation. (Bandyopadhyay viii)

Scandal in Fairyland, which appears a fairytale outwardly, is actually a comedy with a relevant social message. It comprises

Sircar's appraisal of the field of journalism. Here, he attacks people's craving for sensational news-items and shows how unscrupulously media is determined upon providing thrilling accounts of news for the sake of money. It unveils the ugly face of commercialism entered in the field of journalism.

It was first performed on the 18th January 1975 at the Curzon Park, Calcutta by the 'Satabdi' team. In a fairytale framework, Prince Thunderbolt, the hero, goes about killing ogre after ogre and saves eight kingdoms from the doom. It ends on a happy note with a news of Prince Thunderbolt's marriage with Princess Rose, the daughter of Boneyhead Ironheart, the King of Ironia.

The Play's Theme and Story in Brief

The play opens with a newspaper boy, runs in calling people to buy the newspaper *Daily Fairy Green*. He speaks in a 'flamboyant American accent like a caricature of a Chicago gangster' (41). The paper is quite famous as it provides sensational news about Prince Thunderbolt's achievements. As the boy offers special edition without any extra charge, the crowd gathers to collect it. It symbolizes the white collar middle class people's mentality to read anything that is offered free of cost.

It is a story of Prince Thunderbolt who is a slayer of ogres. He has saved six countries so far from the attack of the ogre. Now, there is a call from Copper Land for immediate attention to carry out his seventh mission. In his unique style, Thunderbolt has killed the seventh ogre also and the ogre's body is said to be cut into pieces "and scattered over the seven seas at the ends of the earth, and not a sign of the beast remains, except in the blood stains on the Prince's victorious sword" (42), so read through the *Daily Fairy Green* Version. It is informed through the newspaper, to save his kingdom from the attack of the ogre the King of Ironia, Boneyhead Ironheart, offers half of his kingdom and the hand of his daughter Princess Rose and Prince Thunderbolt remains successful in this mission as usual. The Prince, who has declined the offers of the seven princesses and instead has gained an equivalent value in gold till, now accepts

Princess Rose's proposal to people's surprise. It is declared that their marriage would take place within eight days.

However, the editorial of *Daily Fairy Green* turns the tables on Prince Thunderbolt, since he refuses to be a pawn. The public agitation is raised by the sensational information that the Prince has not killed any ogre as such. To increase the sale of the paper, it has been used as a strategy. The Prince is asked to produce a proof of the death of the ogre. On seeing the turbulence of the people, the King is about to declare emergency. However, Prince Thunderbolt saves the situation by being ready for the public trial. He produces two witnesses, a weeping, harmless old Ogre and a greedy, selfish, shrewd and cunning proprietor of *Daily Fairy Green* Midas Speculatorotti.

The characters of Ogre and that of Midas are juxtaposed. The Ogre, though a monster, is presented as gentle in appearance and behaviour. He is tamed by the Prince and is transformed into a purely vegetarian creature. So, the Prince has saved the kingdoms not by killing the ogres but by changing the mind-set of the mortal brute. Midas used to take thirty-five percent commission to publish the false sensational news regarding Prince Thunderbolt's achievement of saving the kingdom. Despite his trickery, Thunderbolt is forgiven for he has saved many kingdoms from the troubles of the Ogre anyhow.

The play ends on a happy note with the news that Midas, the greedy proprietor of the newspaper leaves for Bengal, Princess Rose getting married with Prince Thunderbolt and the newspaper boy announcing that he too is going to Bengal.

Critical Interpretation and Appraisal of the Play

The matter on the blurb of the textbook hints at the theme of the play succinctly. "In *Scandal in Fairyland*, a street-smart newspaper boy vends the *Daily Fairy Green*, which carries news of the heroic Prince Thunderbolt, who is a champion at beheading ogres which threaten kingdoms. As the action unfolds, we discover wheels within wheels, double-dealing and behind-the-scene fixing, It all, however, ends happily in true fairytale fashion." (Sircar, Blurb)

Scandal in Fairyland can be looked upon as an allegory. Through the creation of the character of the Ogre, Sircar teaches the masses the process of tackling violence. Following the path of non-violence and love, Prince Thunderbolt overpowers the Ogre who is made vegetarian, docile, disciplined and civilized as well.

The play offers a fine blend of a fairytale and the Third Theatre. Like a fairytale, the play has a thrilling element in its story. However, in its performance and dialogues, it follows the Third Theatre convention. Bandyopadhyay narrates, "While *Scandal in Fairyland* in a children's theatre easily lends itself to colourful fairytale glitter, Sircar, for his own performances in the park made his actors/actresses appear in everyday clothes, with a tag on their backs identifying the King, the Minister, the Messenger, etc. The first actor who played Prince Thunderbolt had a large, towering figure and presence, but when he left the group, he was replaced by an actress who appeared in salwar and kameez, her hair tucked under the collar of the kameez and the tag on her back identifying her as Vajrakumar" (Bandyopadhyay viii). The major characters have names and the members of the chorus have numbers. Princess Rose and the Queen totally remain off-stage characters. The circular dialogues and utterances typical of the Third Theatre emphasise the absurdity in the field of media.

The names of characters symbolise their nature. The King is referred to as Boneyhead Ironheart. He is neither diplomatic nor wise. Midas, the proprietor of *Daily Fairy Green* is a replica of the legendary King Midas, quite notorious for his greedy nature. The climax is achieved in the name of the Prince Thunderbolt. It has a mythological reference. Thunderbolt is the deadliest weapon made up of the bones of a great sage Dadhichi, who willingly sacrificed his life for the cause of the good. The name of the Princess is Rose who is narrated to be lovely, educated, gentle, honey-voiced, and sincere in royal duties. The names of the countries such as Gold Landis, Silver State, Pearl Kingdom, Diamond Isle, Emeraldia, Land of Gems, Copper Land and Ironia—indicate their wealthy status. It serves two purposes: It creates the glamour of the fairy tale and it echoes the materialism of the modern world.

The newspaper boy functions like a *sutradhara* and also as a connecting link between the fairyland and the real world. Like the *sutradhara*, he narrates the story, introduces the main characters, passes comments on their actions, and highlights the courageous role of Prince Thunderbolt. In his apparently objective observations, the audience can study the characters and can guess the future state of action. "The character of Prince Thunderbolt is evolved only from the newspaper version and the discussions of the chorus and never from his direct presence until the climax. He appears before the audience only at the end in the trial scene." (Shodhganga 165)

Apparently, the play *Scandal in Fairyland* seems like a fairytale. However, it provides Sircar's scathing criticism on the field of journalism, which is characterised by the corrupting influence of money. While comparing the play with the original version of the story of Premendra Mitra, Samik Bandyopadhyay has quoted his conversation with Sircar, where in the playwright states: "If I had written it for children, I could not have used the idiom of the popular press so extensively." Bandyopadhyay further states: "But Mitra's modern fairytale of a Prince virtually created by the Press and an ogre made to compromise and play a shady 'dying and vanishing' game closely monitored by the Press, only to be exposed at the end by the Press itself, is a brilliant critique of the media in their machinations for sensation and money. Mitra called his press baron Isaac Kuberram Phatkabaaj, and, sentenced to exile, he merely has him (to) say, 'Give me the price for my forty percent. Let me get back to the stock market with that.' Sircar prefers to send him to Bengal." (Bandyopadhyay viii)

The play's ending with the newspaper boy declaring: "Hot scoop! Ironia News—Thunderbolt and Rose wedding.... Yes sir, the *Daily Fairy Green* has folded up. I swear this rotten government paper doesn't sell at all. Dart! I'd better go along to Bengal too. I betcha Midas has brought out a nice, juicy, quick-selling paper there already!" (58)

The play is open-ended. The newspaper boy's action of following in the footsteps of the Editor for the sake of money signifies the unending corruption in the field of media. It ends with a note that the show of exploitation of the feelings of the common people in the fairyland of the mass-media by its scandals will be continued forever.

Works Cited

Bandyopadhyay, Samik. Introduction. *Beyond the Land of Hattamala* and *Scandal in Fairyland*, by Badal Sircar. Seagull, 2003.

Sircar, Badal. Blurb. *Beyond the Land of Hattamala* and *Scandal in Fairyland*. Seagull, 2003.

httpshodhganga.inflibnet.ac.inbitstream10603214431010_chapter%204.pdf.

(N.B. All the textual quotations are from Sircar, Badal. *Beyond the Land of Hattamala, Scandal in Fairyland*. Seagull, 2003.)

15

Beyond the Land of Hattamala: Sircar's Utopia

Introduction

Beyond the Land of Hattamala, originally *Hattamalar Oparey*, that is 'Beyond Topsy-Turvy Land' written in 1977 is a light-hearted 'folk' play or fairytale with a moral or a message. It is a close adaptation of *Hattamalar Deshey*, a novel by Premendra Mitra and Leela Majumdar. Sircar recalls that he had read only a few of the *Sandesh* instalments (the novel is converted into children's magazine), and that had been enough to spark him off. (Bandyopadhyay viii-ix)

The Play's Theme and Story in Brief

It is the story of two young thieves Kenaram and Becharam, Kena and Becha in short, who jump into a river to escape being caught as they run away from angry villagers after a robbery. They find themselves in a new land, which is unfamiliar to them. It is a fairytale world with a lovely garden—a world where peace, happiness and unity prevail. Crime, police abuse and aggression of all kinds are unknown to this world. In this new land, buying and selling are alien concepts. Here, all people work together to produce what the entire community needs. People are rather ignorant of the word 'money', 'cash', 'shop', etc. Kena and Becha do not understand the concept of 'no-money' and hence, several humorous misadventures follow as they make their journey through this land. They enjoy themselves with sweet tender coconut water, a full meal with chilled sweet yogurt and perfectly ripe bananas, jackfruit—all free of cost!

Being thieves, Kena and Becha remain stick to their practice and make a hole through the wall of eatery where they had their free meal. Instead of being angry, the villagers consider them architects and praise them for their accuracy in making the hole. They wonder why Kena and Becha have not used the front gate to enter and to take whatever they wanted to. Even in the jewellery shop, anything can be borrowed and can be used as long as one wants to. All the things in all shops are free. Moreover, they are kept on open shelves for easy replacement.

Kena and Becha remain puzzled why the villagers do not get annoyed to their adversities and how all the things in this land are free of cost. The wise doctor removes their confusion telling them: "No. It isn't really free. We all work to the best of our abilities. That's why we get everything we need" (37). Through this enlightenment, they come to know "Man has to work" (36) and that work is workshop. The thieves, obviously, reform and get themselves busy with jobs, Becha, as a gardener and Kena, as a builder, that is, also as per their wish.

Critical Interpretation and Appraisal of the Play

Sircar is committed to the cause of making people conscious of their social and political conditions. He has used theatre as a means of bringing reformation in the thinking modes of people. In both the plays, *Scandal in Fairyland* and *Beyond the Land of Hattamala*, he draws on the element of fantasy to bring out his concept of a dream-world. However, both the plays have contemporary relevance. In the first one, 'money' plays a vital role in the life of man, which ultimately leads to the creation of corrupt world and in the second one, 'man's hard work' plays a vital role and it naturally leads to the creation of an ideal world. "The avarice for possession of wealth producing fraudulent people in *Scandal in Fairyland* and the rejection of the concept of money or private property, leading to equality and plenty thereby creating an ideal world in *Beyond the Land of Hattamala* are proffered through comic situations which have contemporary relevance." (Shodhganga 163)

The plays are intended specifically neither for children nor for adults. By the means of humour, Sircar seems to give some serious message to all human beings. Samik Bandyopadhyay states: "They have adult themes but children should become aware of these.... In the theatre which Sircar has served all these years..., he has pursued simplicity in theatrical means and ideas alike, in his urge to take theatre to the people to conscientize them to social change with a missionary dedication to the cause of propagating the essential values of a revolutionary project. In both these texts—Sircar exposes politics to its bare bones—and at a level where it has the same message to offer to adults and children alike." (Bandyopadhyay x)

The world would be, as stated by Rabindranath Tagore, a "Heaven of Freedom", if each one follows the Marxian principle "from each according to his capacities, and to each according to his needs". Sircar has dealt with this theme in his earlier play *Prastab* also but in a different way. He has narrated to Samik Bandyopadhyay, "I was upholding a possibility that I had projected in my earlier *Prastab* (Proposal) with almost missionary zeal. At a time when defining Communism anew almost looks like a counter-revolutionary act, I have overheard people in a village discussing the play after a performance and saying, 'Well, there's no reason why it can't be like that!' If we can set people thinking, isn't that the most we can achieve?" (Bandyopadhyay ix). The ideal world of Sircar in *Beyond the Land of Hattamala* establishes a society based on the principles of liberty, equality, fraternity, love, compassion, and concern for fellow human beings without the consideration of wealth. The contrast in this dream-world and the real world is brought out by the characters of the villagers and that of the thieves. The doctor's thinking manifests the merits of the life in Utopia and that of Kena's, the demerits of the real world. However, the words of the doctor bring about a gradual but definite change in the attitudes of both Kena and Becha which is evinced through their decisions of not leading a life of parasite and accepting the work of a builder and a gardener, respectively. Due to the sincerity, love of the people in this utopian land, the thieves are converted into gentle citizens. They willingly join hands with the chorus who sings the significance of combined effort:

> Whatever we need in this world, whatever,
> We can make it all if we work together...
> Come let us share everything together. (38)

The basis of the play is the novel of Premendra Mitra and Leela Majumdar, serialized in the children's magazine *Sandesh*, edited by Nalini Das and Satyajit Ray but it differs from it on many aspects. Sircar himself clarifies it: "I started off from a children's story published in a magazine but the content of the story was changed in the play" (Sircar 122). The play ends with a note that the thieves convert themselves to the culture of that ideal country. In the original novel, the thieves, who are reformed, return to their own village and start leading the life of the citizens in the community. Unlike the play, the novel is lacking in optimistic ending in that the novelists show the thieves often going away in the search of that ideal world but remaining unsuccessful in the task, returning somewhat depressed. The play's ending with the thieves happily joining the song of the chorus is very noteworthy enough signifying that human beings are living in the Utopia following the principle that here, each and every individual gets according to his/her capacity and necessity. Thus, the play differs from its source in its purpose. Enlightenment through entertainment is the prime motto of the playwright. Thinking from this perspective, Anjum Katyal, opines: "The two lovable thieves Kena and Becha (Buy and Sell) who land up accidentally in a Utopian land where no one needs money, and therefore, no one needs to steal, find their noses sadly of joint until they too see the benefits of this humane social system. Full of funny situations and comic moments, it is a delightful play on a thought-provoking subject." (Katyal 93-94)

The play has a fairytale base with humour as its medium but it follows the convention of the third theatre. The central characters, that is, the thieves have names and other characters have just numbers. They also function as the chorus and perform various actions such as the cow, trees, river, door, wall, hole in the wall, etc. The dialogues are colloquial and signify more than what they literally mean.

Majority of Sircar's plays depict the dark, pessimistic side of human life with an intention to make people aware of them, to think over them and to find solutions to them. They aim at creating an egalitarian society. *Beyond the Land of Hattamala* shows Sircar's dream of that ideal society, where all people work for the welfare of humanity, where there is a least consideration for 'money' the most corrupting influence in human life. His love and affection for this play is reflected, when he states: "I would still like to be able to write a play of that kind, but it probably happens once in a lifetime" (Sircar 122). He also tells Bandyopadhyay "This is one of those plays, in which I take genuine pride." (Bandyopadhyay ix)

Scandal in Fairyland and *Beyond the Land of Hattamala* are the only plays of Sircar, where he draws material from adaptation. Otherwise, his plays are based on his acute observation of the contemporary society. Similarly, his plays, being absurd in nature, have no plot, no story, no characterization. While writing *Baki Itihas*, he has stated: "I can never invent stories. Practically no play of mine has a story, for the simple reason that I can't write stories" (Sircar, qtd. in Anjum 61). From this perspective, these two plays mark a little but definite break with Sircar's canon.

To conclude the discussion in Sircar's own words: "*Beyond the Land of Hattamala* works equally well in the Anganmanch and the open air, in towns and in villages, with adults and with children. The subject is ultimate desired and envisioned form of society, where each will work according to his ability and will receive according to his requirements, thereby rendering the use of money unnecessary.... *Hattamalar Oparey* is much more easily performed and has much wider appeal. So far we had 136 performances and it is still going strong." (Sircar 122)

Works Cited

Bandyopadhyay, Samik. Introduction. *Beyond the Land of Hattamala, Scandal in Fairyland*, by Badal Sircar, Seagull, 2003.

httpshodhganga.inflibnet.ac.inbitstream10603214431010_chapter%204.pdf.

Sircar, Badal. *On Theatre*. Seagull, 2009.

Katyal, Anjum. *Badal Sircar: Towards a Theatre of Conscience*. Sage, 2015.

Sircar, PNP, i.e., Badal Sircar speaking at 'Plays in a National Perspective', Round Table-I, 28-30 November 1996, organized by Natya Shodh Sanstha (NSS) at the Bharatiya Bhasha Parishad Conference Room, Kolkata. Quoted in Anjum Katyal.

(N.B. All the textual quotations are from Sircar, Badal. *Beyond the Land of Hattamala, Scandal in Fairyland*. Seagull, 2003).

Epilogue

16

Badal Sircar as a New Playwright

The first Bengali playwright who has transformed the regional theatre into the national theatre is Badal Sircar. Ella Dutta is quite justified in pointing out; "He stands at the forefront of a new theatre movement in India" (Dutta 1). The well-known theatre critic Adya Rangacharya praises Sircar as a playwright who "has breathed new life into the Bengali theatre" (Rangacharya 147). He is an extraordinary, committed artist who views his theatre as a form of social work. He is the founder-director of the most inventive Bengali theatre group "Satabdi". He has directed plays for the conventional stage during the fifties and the sixties before pioneering, in the early seventies, what he calls the Third Theatre with the aim of awakening the urban audience to an awareness of exploitation in rural India and the rural audience to a sense of its power. According to Rustom Bharucha, "Sircar is the only director of creating a genuine people's theatre—a theatre supported and created by the people and not merely performed for the people." (Bharucha 188)

It is observed that Sircar has given a new dimension to the Indian theatre. His plays disturb the audience by raising complex issues that remain unsettled even today in the contemporary society. It is the universal nature of his plays that gives him a place of pride in Indian theatrical scenario.

Sircar is the great social activist who wants to bring about a change in the mind-set of people. He is a committed writer who has devoted his life for the cause of social reformation for making people aware of the problems of their day-to-day life and rendering them to ponder over the situation. "What he wishes to communicate through his theatre are the clear-cut facts, concrete truths about what is happening in the villages, the nature of exploitation both industrial and agricultural, the urban stranglehold on the rural economy.... Not wishing to create new myths in the place of old, he would rather raise people's consciousness and create awareness." (Dutta 4-5)

In Sircar's plays, we have a glimpse of such great western playwrights as Camus, Sartre, Osborne, Becket, Schechner, Grotowski, and Brecht. His plays emphasize the central principle of existentialist philosophy; "Existence precedes essence.... Man first of all exists, encounters himself afterwards.... Man is nothing else but that what he makes of himself" (Asolkar 18). Like Sartre, the Old Man in the play *Procession*, tries to communicate to Khoka:

> To be is to live. To live is to act and to act is to choose and to choose is to invent values and to invent values is to be responsible and to be responsible is to be moral. (Asolkar 18)

Thus, his plays make people aware of their responsibility and ultimately lead them towards new moral consciousness. That is why Khoka joins the procession—the procession of men, the procession that shows the way to a new home.

Evam Indrajit, according to Eakambaram "is an Indian version of *Waiting for Godot*" (Qtd. in Babu 95). The character of Indrajit, like Osborne's Jimmy Porter, represents the angry young man who is not satisfied with the contemporary life but can do nothing against it. The play ends with his realization that he is not different from others and life remains the same in the foreign countries as in India. This realization renders him frustrated since all his efforts, to prove himself Indrajit, (i.e., different from Amal, Vimal, and Kamal) become senseless, absurd, and useless. And he accepts the fact that he is Nirmal. Like Beckett's two tramps, he is walking continuously...with his boredom, his fear of pain. He is a surprisingly effective version of the whole human condition for which action is no answer (Bamber 5). Indrajit's walking constantly, refusing to accept reality, is ridiculous and poignant. It throws light on the absurdity of contemporary life. Reality has been ignored too long to recall. The play ends where it starts. It symbolizes the fact that human life starts and ends in "Sartrian" Being and Nothingness.

Bertolt Brecht reacted against the Aristotelian theatre and introduced Epic Theatre to help the audience remain critically aware. To incorporate several issues at the same time, he took the help of various devices like projectors, slides, masks, etc. Sircar never uses the technical devices integral to the Epic dramaturgy. But the effect, he intends to attain is quite similar to that of the Epic Theatre. Subhendu Sarkar points out:

> Direct communication with the audience, making eye contact with them, at times whispering in their ears and on certain occasions almost touching them help the spectators to remain conscious that they are watching a dramatic performance. Therefore, what Brecht attends through *Verfremdungseffekt*, Sircar attends to achieve through direct communication with the audience. Brecht and Sircar might walk different paths but it is same destination that both of them are bound for. (Sarkar xxxvi)

It is noticed that Sircar's plays mark a sharp break with the conventional, well-made plays. Although they explore the absurdity of human life, they neither look nonsensical nor seek to provide a boisterous laughter. Instead, they evoke contempt, sadness, and anguish in the audience at human absurdities. Majority of the plays have no story, no plot, no action, and no characterization, but they have a great deal that needs to be understood. The dialogues, apparently incoherent though they are, signify more than what they say. Thus, the plays aim to stimulate thought on a wider range of issues and not to just preach morals or values.

Most of Sircar's plays aim at giving the crude banality of social life a dramatic garb. He projects life as it is with all its challenges, difficulties and complexities. In the depiction of life, his attention is focused not on the happy, gleeful aspects of life but on its vices, drawbacks, and weaknesses. He intends to make people introspective and sensitive to the issues of life. In this sense, Sircar appears to be a social activist who desires to bring about a change in people's mode of thinking, feeling, and behaving.

Sircar uses drama to ask questions rather than to provide answers. In his plays, one can clearly see his keen observation of life. The events and incidents depicted in the play have their origin in real life. Although pessimism characterizes most of his plays, one notices that there is a streak of optimism almost in every play. That is why Indrajit in *Evam Indrajit* chooses to be on the road; Khoka in *Procession* joins the procession thinking that it is the procession of dream, a procession—showing the way to new home; the play *Stale News* ends with a the actor (ONE) demanding the audience: "Why don't you scream? Is it still not time? Not time?" (163) It strikes a note of hope that—A revolution will be born of exploitation, oppression, and injustice to actualize the dream of Santhals 'who dream of and die for the emergence of a new and better society' (Sircar, Letter 53). Similarly, the play *Bhoma* ends with Bhoma and other people cutting down the forest of poisonous trees. Although Sircar tries his best to remain a detached observer, his optimism can be perceived through such characters as Writer in *Procession* and the Old Man in *Stale News*. These characters appear to be their creator's mouthpieces.

Sircar can also be seen as an avant-garde playwright in realistic strain for he deliberately undertakes, in Ezra Pound's phrase 'to make it new' (Abrams 120). He had shocked the sensibility of the conventional, traditional readers by revolting against the accepted norms and values and by introducing neglected and sometimes forbidden subject-matters. A direct confrontation with banality, sordidness, vulgar reality, and violence is difficult for the audience to bear. It gives the audience such a jerk that they are lulled out of their unconsciousness. They become introspective. So, their outlook gets broadened, sensibility gets sharpened, and vision becomes clear. "...What Erin B. Mee states in her introduction to the *Drama*

Contemporary, she has edited, very-well applies to the Sircar plays:

> I hope that each play take people on a journey... however, the journey need not be to India: It can be a journey into one's self from a stance outside one's own cultural viewpoint. (Mee 18)

Sircar is interested more in the direction and performance of the play rather than in the writing of the play. He states: "I say this truthfully, I am not a playwright,... I am a theatre man" (Sircar, Interview 208). And he dismisses his contribution to theatre writing lightly with the comment:

> I prefer doing theatre to writing theatre. Writing is quite laborious for me.... I started writing plays as a matter of expediency. (Qtd. in Dutta 2)

Sircar's writing, it is observed, is marked by a subtle satirical sense since he explores vices, drawbacks, flaws, and weaknesses of life. The function of his play is not just to entertain, nor just to reveal irony and contradictions but to help man introspect and know himself in relation to his environment. About *Bhoma*, he states: "*Bhoma* is not a play aiming to entertain the well-dressed front-row audience in a lush theatre. I am sure that those who do that kind of theatre will not touch my play anyway" (Sircar, Preface 58). His aim in writing and performing plays is to transform drama from a means of entertainment into an object of instruction. In other words, he intends to make theatre a medium of higher education. And he succeeds in reaching his goal. In his article "Voyages in the Theatre", Sircar noted his experience after the performance of the play *Bhoma* in a village. A group of labourers came to meet the team. The headmaster of the school asked them: 'What they thought of the play and whether they understood it;' he tried to provoke them by saying that it did not seem likely, with no story, no costumes, no songs—nothing in fact, that made theatre interesting. This labourer I was talking about thought for a moment, and then answered coolly, "There was nothing in the play that we poor people would find it difficult to understand, maybe the rich would find difficult to understand it." (Sircar, *On* 117)

The greatest contribution of Sircar to Indian theatre is his Third Theatre. He uses it as a tool of social change and not simply as an expression of his innovative techniques. Subhendu Sarkar opines: "Badal Sircar is the pioneer of an alternative theatre movement in India that continues to work without government and commercial aid, without advertising in the newspapers and, above all, without falling into the trap of the money economy. It thrives with the active support of its own audience and never compromises on its objective: to make people aware of their responsibilities in fighting an unjust system." (Sarkar xxxvii)

It is observed that characters in Sircar's later plays which were written after the formation of the Third Theatre are not individualized at all. They can be seen as what Sircar himself has said: "I can be taken as a prototype of a particular class in a society at a particular period" (Qtd. by Dass 69). The spectator assumes the protagonist's role in the theatre of Sircar making the theatrical incident experimental, indeterminate, and open-ended. (Dass 69)

It is observed that the beginning of realistic theatre started in Bengal with the plays of Utpal Dutt. Sircar's contribution to this realistic theatre was to help it to transcend its first over-simplistic message oriented phase for a mature phase that sought to integrate medium into message. Here, realism is not taken to be a naïve representation of historical reality. In this form of theatre, the spectator does not complacently appropriate an image of the present-day world but as in the Epic theatre of Brecht through the use of the technical device of montage the action is interrupted preventing both empathy and illusions. So, the attempt here is not to depict the present-day world but rather to expose it.

Though Sircar has adopted Brecht's concept of Epic theatre, the realism represented in Sircarian dramaturgy is distinct from that of represented in Brecht's plays. His theatre is close to the Brechtian 'estrangement effect' but it differs from it from the point of view of the participation of the spectators. His idea of taking the participation of the audience through the progressive use of the theatrical space, places him and his theatre directly into the tradition of Artaud, Grotowski and Schechner. So, Brecht's theatre demands 'distance' plus 'reflection' whereas Sircar's theatre demands 'distance' plus 'participation'. As pointed out by Pronoti Chukerbutty: "Here the meaning has to be arrived at not just mentally but through physical participation as well" (Chukerbutty 107). She continued her conclusions on Sircar's contribution with a justified statement: "Sircar can be considered to be among those writers who have successfully transcribed the structures of their society without ostensibly, subscribing to any group or party positions." And throughout this enterprise, he "maintains a studied independence that allows his artistic temperament to flower without party dictates enforcing artistic compliance." (Chukerbutty 108)

It is Sircar, who makes theatre 'people's theatre'. It is because of him, that drama reaches villages where eighty percent of India's people live. Due to his technique of making theatre inexpensive, the poor people become the audiences of theatre. The plays help them to become conscious of their exploitation, oppression, and suppression and to find out the remedies.

Although Sircar depicts the dark side of life, his commitment to human values can be easily perceived in his plays. The plays present the society divided on the basis of caste, class, colour, religion, etc. Inequality, corruption, and violence characterize it. The life projected in the plays is full of contradictions and miserable, but it is real. The plays indirectly throw light on the fact that the dramatist has a desire to strive tirelessly for perfection of life. He wants to create an egalitarian society based on equality, social justice, freedom, and fraternity. This dream finds expression in his play *Beyond the Land of Hattamala*. Sircar believes in the Marxian credo: "For each according to his ability, to each according to his needs" (Ramnarayan 75) which expresses both, his rationalism and his optimism.

Works Cited

Abrams, M.H. *A Glossary of Literary Terms*. Prism, 1993.

Asolkar, Sharad. "Astitwawad ani Sartre." *Yugwani*, edited by Sharad Kolarkar, May, 1980.

Babu, Manchi Sarat. *Indian Drama Today: Study in the Theme of Cultural Deformity*. Prestige, 1997.

Bamber, Gascoigne. *Twentieth Century Drama*. Hutchinson, 1962.

Bharucha, Rustom. *Rehearsals of Revolution: The Political Theatre of Bengal*. Seagull, 1983.

Chukerbutty, Pronoti. *Phases in the Development of Realism in Twentieth Century Drama: A Comparative Study of the Theatre in Bengal and Britain*. A Dissertation submitted in partial fulfillment of the requirement for the degree of Master of Letters in English Literature, English and Foreign Languages University, Hyderabad. Sept. 1982.

Dass, Veena Noble. "Experiment and Innovation in Modern Indian Drama in Translation: The Plays of Mohan Rakesh, Badal Sircar, Vijay Tendulkar, and Girish Karnad." *Contemporary Indian Drama*, edited by Sudhakar Pandey and Freya Taraporwala. Prestige, 1990.

Dutta, Ella. Introduction. *Three Plays*, by Badal Sircar, Seagull, 2009.

Mee, Erin B., editor. Introduction. *Drama Contemporary*. OUP, 2002.

Ramnarayan, Gowri. "The Endless Road of Badal Sircar's Free Theatre." *Frontline*, 28 Aug. 1972.

Rangacharya, Adya. *The Indian Theatre*. National Book Trust, 1971.

Sarkar, Subhendu. Introduction. *Two Plays: Indian History Made Easy, Life of Bagala*, by Badal Sircar, OUP, 2010.

Sircar, Badal. Interview with Veena Noble Dass. *Modern Indian Drama in English Translation*. 1988.

———. "A Letter from Badal Sircar." *The Drama Review* (US). Vol. 26, No. 2, Summer, 1982.

———. Preface. *Three Plays*. Seagull, 2009.

Appendix

BADAL SIRCAR/SUDHINDRA SIRCAR

Early Life and Education

Birth	: 15th July 1925, Calcutta (now Kolkata)
Death	: 13th May 1911 due to colon cancer
Education	: Scottish Church Collegiate School, Scottish Church College, Civil Engineering at the Bengal Engineering College (now IIEST), Shibpur, Master of Arts degree in Comparative Literature from the Jadavpur University, Calcutta
Residence	: Manicktala, Kolkata
Active Work	: 1945-2011
Awards	: Sangit Natak Akademi Award-1968, Padma Shri-1972, Ratna Sadsya-1997 (i.e., Sangit Natak Akademi Fellowship—the highest honour in the performing arts by Govt. of Maharashtra). He was offered the Padma Bhushan by the by Govt. of India in 2010, which he declined, stating that he is already a Sahitya Akademi Fellow, which is the highest recognition for a writer.
Career	: While working as a town planner in India, England and Nigeria, he entered theatre as an actor, moved to direction, but soon

started writing plays. Disillusioned with the contemporary form of theatre, he established his own theatre called "Third Theatre" where he minimised the use of sets, props, costumes and also discards the use of mechanical devices like tape-recorders and projectors. This theatre filled the gulf between the performers and the spectators and became "People's Theatre". In 1967, he formed the "Satabdi" theatre group which cooperated him in writing, directing and performing plays. By 1977, he gave up his town plannership and became a full time theatre-man.

Plays

Solution X (1956); *Boro Pishima* (1957); *Shanibar* (1959); *Ram Shyam Jadu* (1961); *Samabritta* (1961); *Ebong Indrajit* (1963); *Sara Rattir* (1963); *Ballabhpurer Rupkatha* (1963-64); *Kabikahani* (1964); *Bichitranushthan* (1964); *Baki Itihas* (1965); *Bagh* (1965); *Porey Konodin* (1966); *Jodi Aar Ekbar* (1966); *Pralap* (1966); *Tringsha Shatabdi* (1966); *Bibar* (1967); *Pagla Ghoda* (1967); *Circus* (1968); *Shesh Nei* (1970); *Sagina Mahato 1* (1970); *Sagina Mahato 2* (1970); *Abu Hossin* (1971); *Spartacus* (1972); *Suitcase* (1972); *Beej* (1973); *Prastab* (1973); *Muktamela* (1973); *Michhil* (1974); *Bhanumati Ka Khel* (1974); *Lakshmicharar Panchali* (1974); *Rupkathar Kelankari* (1974); *Bhoma* (1975); *Sukhapathya Bharoter Itihash* (1976); *Bhanga Manush* (1977); *Hottomalar Oparey* (1977); *Minikanchan* (1977); *Gondi* (1877); *Captain Hurra* (1977); *Badi Buaji* (1977); *Padma Nadir Majhi* (1978); *Basi Khabar* (1978); *Memorandum* (1979); *Ekti Hatyar Natyakatha* (1979); *Naditey* (1980); *Manushe Manushe* (1981); *Nagini Kanya* (1981); *Dwoirath* (1982); *Androcles O Singha* (1982); *Khat Mat Kring* (1983); *Sinri* (1984); *Udyog Parba* (1985); *Janmabhumi Aaj* (1986); *Sada Kalo* (1986); *Churna Prithibi* (1987); *Dampatya* (1987/88); *Baiscope* (1988); *Bhul Rasta* (1988); *Padma Nadir Majhi* (1990); *Yadi Ek Bar Firse* (1990); *Androklis o Singha* (1991); *Charuibhati* (1994); *Ka Cha Ta Ta Pa* (1995); *Bagalcharitmanas* (1997/98); *Andhakar* (1999); *Dairath* (2001); *Nadite* (2002);

Aeschyluser Natak (2002); *Parashuram* (2003); *Ore Bihanga* (2009).

The Third Theatre Plays

Spartacus (1972); *Prastab* (1973); *Muktamela* (Free Fair) (1973); *Michhil* (Procession) (1974); *Bhanumati Ka Khel* (Amazing Magic) (1974); *Lakshmicharar Panchali* (Song of Destitute) (1974); *Rupkathar Kelankari* (Scandal in Fairy Land) (1974); *Bhoma* (1975); *Sukhapathya Bharoter Itihas* (Indian History Made Easy) (1976); *Bhanga Manush* (Broken Humans) (1977); *Hottomalar Oparey* (Beyond the Land of Hattamala) (1977); *Minikanchan* (Mani and Kanchan) (1977); *Gondi* (Circle) (1877); *Captain Hurra* (1977); *Basi Khabar* (Stale News) (1978); *Ekti Hatyar Natyakatha* (Marat/Sade) (Dramatic Version of a Murder) (1979); *Manushe Manushe* (Amongst Humans) (1981); *Nagini Kanya* (The Serpent Girl) (1981); *Khat Mat Kring* (1983); *Sinri* (Stairs) (1984); *Udyog Parba* (War-Preparations) (1985); *Janmabhumi Aaj* (Motherland Today) (1986); *Sada Kalo* (White Black) (1986); *Churna Prithibi* (Frangmented World) (1987); *Baiscope* (Bioscope) (1988); *Bhul Rasta* (Wrong Route) (1988); *Padma Nadir Majhi* (Boatman of River Padma) (1990); *Androklis o Singha* (Androcles and the Lion) (1991); *Charuibhati* (Picnic) (1994); *Ka Cha Ta Ta Pa* (1995); *Bagalcharitmanas* (Life of Bagala) (1997/98); *Dairath* (Duel) (2001); *Nadite* (In the River) (2002); *Ore Bihanga* (O Bird) (2009).

Plays in Translation

Evam Indrajit, translated into English by Girish Karnad, OUP, 1974.

Baki Itihas, edited by Chandrasekhar Kamber, translated into Hindi by Nemichandra Jain, Radhakrishna, 2001.

Beyond the Land of Hattamala and Scandal in Fairy Land, translated into English by Suchanda Sarkar. Seagull, 2003.

Shesh Nei. Modern Indian Plays. Vol. 1, edited by Chandrasekhar Kambar, translated by Sarah K. Ensley, Vol. 1, National School of Drama, pp. 317-97.

Three Plays: Procession, Bhoma, Stale New, translated into English by Samik Bandyopadhyay Seagull, 1985.

Two Plays: Indian History Made Easy, Life of Bagala, translated into English by Subhendu Sarkar, OUP, 2010.

Pagla Ghoda, translated in Marathi by Amol Palekar.

Bhoma, translated into Hindi by the members of the Theatre Workshop such as Sudhir Sudhanshu, Mishra et al., Vidya Prakashan Mandir, 2002.

Badi Buaji, translated into Hindi by Pratibha Agrawal, Rajkamal Prakashan, 1977.

Sari Raat, translated into Hindi by Pratibha Agrawal, Vidya Prakashan Mandir, 1991.

Sagina Mahato 1, translated into Hindi by Shivkumar Zunzunwala, Vidya Prakashan Mandir, 1979.

Yadi Ek Bar Firse, translated into Hindi by Pratibha Agrawal, Kala Prakashan, 1990.

Books by Badal Sircar

On Theatre. Seagull, 2009.

The Changing Language of Theatre. Indian Council for Cultural Relations, 1982.

The Third Theatre. Pioneer, 1992.

Bibliography

Primary Sources

Sircar, Badal. *Baki Itihas*, edited by Chandrasekhar Kamber, translated into Hindi by Nemichandra Jain, Radhakrishna, 2001.

———. *Beyond the Land of Hattamala and Scandal in Fairyland*. Seagull, 2003.

———. *Evam Indrajit,* translated into English by Girish Karnad, OUP, 1974.

———. *On Theatre*. Seagull, 2009.

———. *Shesh Nei*. *Modern Indian Plays*. Vol. 1, edited by Chandrasekhar Kambar, translated by Sarah K. Ensley, National School of Drama, pp. 317-97.

———. *The Changing Language of Theatre*. Indian Council for Cultural Relations, 1982.

———. *The Third Theatre*. Pioneer, 1992.

———. *Three Modern Indian Plays (Karnad, Sircar, Tendulkar)*. OUP, 2009.

———. *Three Plays: Procession, Bhoma, Stale News*. Seagull, 1985.

———. *Two Plays: Indian History Made Easy, Life of Bagala*. OUP, 2010.

Secondary Sources

Abrams, M.H. *A Glossary of Literary Terms*. Macmillan, 2007.

Babu, Sarat Manchi. *Indian Drama Today: Study in the Theme of Cultural Deformity*. Prestige, 1997.

Bamber, Gascoigne. *Twentieth Century Drama*. Hutchson, 1962.

Bharucha, Rustom. *Rehearsals of Revolution: The Political Theatre of Bengal*. Seagull, 1983.

———. *Theatre and the World: Performance and the Politics of Culture*. Routledge, 1993.

Bhatta, S. Krishna. *Indian English Drama: A Critical Study*. Sterling, 1987.

Chakraborty, Kaustav. *Indian Drama in English*. PHI Learning Pvt. Ltd., 2011.

Chattopadhyay, Kuntal. *Third Theatre*. Ratnabali, 2002.

Deshpande, L.S. *Samakaleen Bharatiya Rangabhumi* (Contemporary Indian Theatre M.S. in Marathi) Dissertation submitted to K.K. Birla Foundation, 2008.

Deshpande, Sudhanva, editor. *Theatre of the Streets: The Jana Natya Manch Experience*. Leftword Books, 2007.

Dharwadkar, Aparna Bhargava. *Theatres of Independence: Drama, Theory, and Urban Performance in India Since 1947*. University of Iowa Press, 2005.

Dodiya, J.K., and K.V. Surendran, editors. *Indian English Drama: Critical Perspectives*. Sarup and Sons, 2000.

Esslin, Martin. *Theatre of the Absurd*. Penguin, 1968.

Gagri, Balwant. *Theatre in India*. Theatre Arts, 1962.

Gaskell, Ronald. *Drama and Reality*. Routledge and Kegan Paul, 1972.

Gowda, Anniah. *Indian Drama*. University of Mysore, 1974.

Kanwar, Asha S. *The Theatre of* India, translated by Mukherji Narayan, 2 Vols., Writers' Workshop, 1978.

Katyal, Anjum. *Badal Sircar: Towards a Theatre of Conscience*. Sage, 2015.

Levi, Sylvain. *The Theatre of India*, translated by Mukherji Narayan, Writers' Workshop, 1978.

Pandey, Sudhakar, and Freya Barua, editors. *New Directions in Indian Drama*. Prestige, 1994.

Pandey, Sudhakar, and Freya Taraporwala, editors. *The Studies in Contemporary Indian Drama*. Prestige, 1990.

Prasad A.N., et al., editors. *Studies in Indian Drama in English*. Prakash Book Depot, 2003.

Raha, Kironmoy. *Bengali Theatre*. National Book Trust, India, 1978.

Rangacharya, Adya. *Introduction to Bharata's Natyasastra*. Popular Prakashan, 1966.

———. *The Indian Theatre*. Sahitya Akademi, 1971.

Reddy, Bayapa P. *Studies in Indian Writing in English with a Focus on Indian English Drama*. Prestige, 1990.

Schechner, Richard. *Performative Circumstances: From the Avant-Garde to Ramlila*. Seagull, 1983.

———. *Environmental Theatre*. Applause Books, 1994.

Tandon, Neeru, editor. *Perspectives and Challenges in India English Drama*. Atlantic, 2006.

Tiwari, Shubha, editor. *Contemporary Indian Dramatists*. Atlantic, 2007.

Vatsyaya, Kapila. *Traditional Indian Theatre: Multiple Streams*. National Book Trust, 1980.

Dissertations, Articles, Interviews, and Introductions

Anniah Gowda, H.H. "Indian Drama in English: Some Highlights." *Indian Writing in the New Millennium*, edited by R.K. Dhawan, IAES, 1999.

Babu, Sarat Manchi. "Theatre Log: A Retrospective of Badal Sircar's Plays." *Seagull Theatre Quarterly*, 8 December, 1995.

Bandyopadhyay, Samik. "Theatrescapes." *Seagull Theatre Quarterly*, 16 December, 1997.

———. Introduction. *Beyond the Land of Hattamala and Scandal in Fairyland*, by Badal Sircar, Seagull, 2003.

Banerjee, Arundhati. "Brecht Adaptations in Modern Bengali Theatre: A Study in Reception." *Asian Theatre Journal*, 7 (1): 1-28, Spring, 1990.

Banerjee, Paramita. "Street Theatre in Bengal: A Glimpse." *Seagull Theatre Quarterly*, 16 December, 1997.

———. "*Pagla Ghoda*: A Review." *Seagull Theatre Quarterly*, 11, September, 1996.

Banerjee, Sumanta. "The Theatre of Badal Sircar." *Theatre India*, No. 2, November, 1999.

Banfild, Chris, and Brain Crow. "Badal Sircar's Third Theatre of Kolkata." *An Introduction to Post-Colonial Theatre*. Cambridge University Press, 1996.

Bhattacharjee, Shampa. *Badal Sircar's Street Plays: A Thematic Study*. An M. Phil. Dissertation submitted to Kakatiya University, Warangal, 1994.

Bhatta, Krishna S. "Indo-Anglian Drama: A Critical Study." *Triveni*, 52.3, 1983.

———. "Indian English Drama: Models and Techniques." *Triveni*, 56.2, 1987.

Dhawan, R.K. "New Directions in Indian Drama: A Report on the Seminar." *New Directions in Indian Drama*, edited by Sudhakar Pandey and Freya Barua, Prestige, 1994.

Dubey, Satyadev, and Vijay Tendulkar. Introduction. *Three Modern Indian Plays*. OUP, 1989.

Dutta, Ella. Introduction. *Three Plays*, by Badal Sircar, Seagull, 2009.

Gunawardana, A.J. "Problems and Directions: Calcutta's New Theatre." *The Drama Review*, 1971.

Harrison, Jane. "From Ritual to Art." *Sociology of Literature and Drama*, edited by Tom Burns and Elizabeth Burns, Penguin, 1973.

Hemadri, Usha. "The Relevance of Experimental Theatre." *Indian Post*. 6, 2 July 1989.

Iyer, Natesan Sharda. "Badal Sircar: *Evam Indrajit*: An Overview." *Musing on Indian Writing in English Drama*. Sarup and Sons, 2007.

Katyal, Anjum. "Distance, Access, Control: The Philosophy of Space in Badal Sircar." *Beyond the Proscenium: Reimagining the Space for Performance*, edited by Anmol Vellani, IFA Theatre Infrastructure Cell, 2010.

Lal, Ananda. "Badal Sircar." *The Oxford Encyclopedia of Theatre and Performance,* Vol. 2, edited by Dennis Kennedy, Oxford University Press, 2003.

Luykx, Nicolaas. "A Public Policy Profile on Rural Development in Bengal." *Aspects of Bengali History and Society*, edited by Rachel Van M. Baumer, Vikas, 1976.

Marulasiddappa, K. "Drama's Turning Point." *Spectrum*, translated by Chaitanya, 11 Jun., 1994.

Menon, Sadanand. "Towards a People Theatre." *The Sunday Observer*, Sept. 30, 1984.

Moses, Sudha. *Anger and Commitment in the Post-War British Drama.* A Ph.D. Dissertation, submitted to the Marathwada University, Aurangabad, 1970.

Pandit, Maya. "A Dark Continent: Modernity and Gender: Perception in Modern Indian Theatre." *Theatre India*, No. 17, May 2003.

Raha, Kironmoy. "Quest for Modernity." *Theatre India*, 5 May 2002.

———. "The Other Theatre." *Bengali Theatre.* National Book Trust of India, 1978.

Rai, R.N. "Perspectives and Challenges in Indian English Drama." *Perspectives and Challenges in Indian English Drama*, edited by Neeru Tandon, Atlantic, 2006.

Sen, Aditya. "The Bengali Literary Scene." *Indian Literature,* 17(4): 20-29, October-December, 1974.

Shiva Prakash, H.S. "Here and Now: The Search for the New in Indian Drama and Theatre." *Indian Literature,* Vol. 44, No. 1 (195) January-February 2000.

Sircar, Badal. "A Letter from Badal Sircar." *The Drama Review* (US). Vol. 26, No. 2, Summer, 1982.

———. "Voyages in the Theatre." *On Theatre.* Seagull, 2009.

Sarkar, Subhendu. Introduction. *Two Plays: Indian History Made Easy, Life of Bagala*, by Badal Sircar, OUP, 2010.

Shukla, Supriya. "Indian English Drama: An Introduction." *Perspective and Challenges in Indian-English Drama*, edited by Neeru Tandon, Atlantic, 2006.

Yadav, Saryug. "Indian English Drama: Tradition and Achievement." *Indian English Drama: Critical* Perspectives, edited by J.K. Dodiya and K.V. Surendran. Sarup and Sons, 2000.

Yarrow, Ralph. "Alternative Practitioners and Theatre of Development." *Indian Theatre: Theatre of Origin, Theatre of Freedom*. Curzon Press, 2001.

Online Sources

http://shodhganga.inflibnet.ac.in/bitstream/10603/21443/8/08_chapter%202.pdf

httpshodhganga.inflibnet.ac.inbitstream10603214431010_chapter%2

http://shodhganga.inflibnet.ac.in/bitstream/10603/21443/8/08_chapter%202.pdf

http://www.expressindia.com/ie/daily/19991020/ile20071.html

http.hinduonnet.com

http:www.hindunnet.com/thehindu/2001/09/16/stories/1416288.htm

http://www.meadev.nic.in/culture/theatre/modern.htm

www.vedambooks.com

Index